MARYANN CAMACHO

How Many Employees Does It Take To Change A Lightbulb?

The art of empowering your team to make transformational change

D1714054

First edition

ISBN: 9798859411276

Editing by Hugh Barker

This book was professionally typeset on Reedsy.
Find out more at reedsy.com

To our son, Zachary: May you be, and work, in the company of greatness.

Contents

Preface

As leaders, we know change is necessary and constant. In order to gain a competitive edge, we must both initiate transformations AND successfully finish them. However, change can be daunting, messy, and full of risk. Is there a magic wand we can use to make it easier? Probably not. However, I have found a common element among successful leaders: **They respect the intellect of their frontline and engage them in innovating the company.** I know the skills can be taught and a team culture can be shaped. I believe I have figured out a repeatable way to make constant change, successfully, and want to show you how to do the same with your team.

I have over 30 years of professional experience working from frontline roles to boardroom reviews. In my early engineering days I fixed magnetic resonance equipment. In my executive years I fixed multi-billion dollar business operations. I continually strive to be an avid learner of contemporary change for business operations. I am a self-professed process junkie who loves continuous improvement work. When I realized a few years ago that my natural leadership tendency was to go to the frontline to engage in transformation, I knew this was what I was meant to do in life. It is my pleasure to share proven business operations leadership techniques to light up the intellect of your employees and the needs of your customers.

There are many great examples of companies who have demonstrated excellence in this realm. Their similarity seems to be a fantastic culture that fosters an amazing employee and customer experience[1]. Some of my favorites are Zappos, Costco, Quest Diagnostics, Wegmans, and Cisco. Unfortunately, there are many other companies that churn and burn employees and leave customers underwhelmed. In comparing the employee churners and the culture cultivators, another factor of transformational success appears to be in the companies with innovation, prosperity, and downright fun at work. They have leaders who recognize human intellect is limitless and powerful. They know happy employees lead to happy customers, which leads to a profitable business. They do more than just have hope in their employees though. Great leaders learn how to harness great employee experiences in the teams they lead. They do it whether they are working side by side, or virtually via a computer screen.

If you are mired in layoffs and numerous other cost-cutting programs, take a moment to let me open your eyes to an alternative way of achieving lasting prosperity. Let's start with a few questions. Do you believe in your team? Do you wish you could make a transformational business decision your team will willingly execute? How many times have you faced a roll of red tape, budget cuts, and exhausting return-on-investment reviews only to be in the same place you started? Do you yearn to make a positive change for your business, but are feeling like a hamster in the proverbial wheel, spinning endlessly to nowhere? Unfortunately, you may have answered yes to one or more of these questions. You probably see so much potential for your team, but also too much gunk in your way. What if there was a way to harness the good stuff to overpower the difficult stuff?

You may have picked up this book to find the answer to my cover question: How many employees does it take to change a lightbulb? Well, the answer depends on many factors including your company culture and leadership style. Whether it is perceived or real, the bureaucracy of corporations can stifle creativity AND productivity in its chain of commanding policies and procedures. Even seemingly simple tasks can take forever to get approved not to mention executed in small and large companies alike. You may have recently been prey to a well-intentioned meeting to brainstorm a solution, set up at exactly 2 p.m. with 50 people on a Zoom session. Right? I mean that's the time of day when we are all at our peak performance, with the creative juices spilling out. Wrong! Most of the time, we could have figured out a way to change the lightbulb, or whatever else, in less than half the time it took to get through the introductions.

Because culture is so important in your ability to make a change, it is important to realize that a culture of innovation and prosperity is cultivated, not scheduled. There are lots of great books about strategies for creating a great work culture. I will reference many of them throughout. Two of my all-time favorites are *The Good Jobs Strategy* (GJS)[2] and *The Case for Good Jobs*[3] by MIT Professor Zeynep Ton. Her proven formula is comprised of simplifying product offerings, empowering employees, cross-training, and operating with slack. The GJS system works, and I am living proof of this. I have witnessed the power of it in leading teams directly. However, many companies struggle to even *start* the journey.

Over the past three decades, working with some of the best corporate leadership development firms and continuous improvement practitioners, I have refined the lessons I learned in leading teams into a set of steps you can easily follow to start transforming your business and make change last. It is applicable to many different business types from manufacturing to retail, government to healthcare, and frontline to back-office service teams. It is an easy-to-understand set of building blocks providing an adaptable and repeatable method of leading teams. It is not a theory. It's real-life, hands-on work, that works.

I refer to the set of blocks as "Model Team Methodology"™. The premise is to focus on one manageable group of people (your "Model Team") at a time, and bring the best ideas forward with some basic structure and operational management, to foster a culture of innovation and prosperity. In short, I found a way to make work that employees actually like to do. I make work fun, and you can too.

The chapters ahead will provide you with a blueprint to achieve stable and scalable operations providing transformative results in your firm. The first half of the book will help you learn **how to engage your team** to be innovative and drive a culture of change. The second half of the book details **how to empower them** to make effective change stick. There are templates in the appendix and on www.modelteamenterprises.com to guide you.

You will find many "Lightbulb Moments" provided throughout this book tagged by a suitable icon. I encourage you to pause, reflect on them and ask yourself, "Am I doing this?"

Model Team Methodology™ is an iterative method of engaging your team. It is a process to make transformational change more manageable and effective. The method came to me when I led the start-up of a circuit board manufacturing plant from a dirt floor warehouse using continuous improvement techniques combined with a heavy dose of humanism. My leadership techniques were further honed as I led commercial operations for a multi-billion-dollar healthcare equipment business processing service contracts and invoices. They were cemented for me when I unified more than 15 call center teams into one super high-performing group. MIT Sloan and Harvard Business Schools have helped me learn a ton along the way and featured my work. I believe I can teach you how to engage and empower your team to make change for good.

Chapter 1

You Win More When Folks Choose to Play... Generating a Groundswell

Let's imagine you are gathered in a conference room when one of your supervisors walks in with a pair of galoshes on and a fishing pole in their hand. It would certainly grab your attention, and you may even notice your staff grinning. If this is how your initial round of Model Team selection goes, you are going to be delighted with the rest of the process. The end result is going to be even better than you expected.

You are here to generate a groundswell for change. Each of your supervisors has been given the rules for a brief presentation they will deliver to you and your team. They have less than a day to prepare their story and no more than five minutes to sell you on why they should be selected as the next Model Team. Their pitch needs to convince you they are ready to be invested in. It is akin to being on ABC's *Shark Tank*[4].

Becoming one of the first groups in the organization to undergo a Model Team transformation will require training, project support, and a change management attitude unlike any they have witnessed before. They have to convey their ideas for making interactions better for customers, not just with problem statements, but proposed solutions to accompany them. They also must assure you they know a little about what they are getting into and that their team is stable enough to move forward. They need to show you they are a leader you can count on to drive change and succeed.

I have to say, anyone willing to come to an executive presentation with the kind of get-up creative minds can dream up is definitely in it to win it. They might start by telling you, "Our team is ready to go 'fishing' for a better way to get things done around here." The room will burst into laughter. You'll continue grinning from ear to ear and reply, "Tell us all about it, you have 4 minutes and 45 seconds left."

Preparation for Change

Imagine what got you here is your decision to take on a large transformation project of operations at your firm. The work leading up to initiating a major change has probably taken you about two months. You'll have spent time assessing the situation by doing interviews and observing work. Then, you lobbied to get some support and help in place to manage the change. You might decide to follow a continuous improvement mantra for step-wise, yet lasting transformation of your operations. You might choose a single continuous improvement leader to start with, and give them part-time support from local resources. Later on, this person may be supported by ambassadors who are skilled in the basic mechanics of change. The leaders I have seen do this knew how to teach and implement tools such as searching for waste and target sheets. What they usually didn't have was leadership support and endorsement for this business unit. That's where you come in.

All the resources in terms of time, money, and people matter diddly-squat if you do not have a leader who wants to change. I have found that even the most passive-aggressive, been there a long time, stuck in the past leaders **do** want to make transformational change. The issue is, they are either afraid of failure, embarrassment, don't know how to do it, or some combination therein. I really like and can relate some of my experiences to the work of the world famous professor, author, and podcast leader Brene Brown. She talks about the role shame plays in our lives in her book, *Dare to Lead*[5]. She says, "The courage to be vulnerable is not about winning or losing, it's about the courage to show up when you can't predict or control the outcome." I call it having guts, and my mother would say the same thing. She was always headstrong like that, and I suppose she passed that down, to me.

Perhaps you see a lack of courage in some of your leaders today. They might be highly experienced and have been hired to start a transformation. Like you, they love and care for their teams. But, somewhere along the way, they might have become afraid of making change truly happen. Why is this you wonder? Are they afraid someone else could come along and question or perhaps might embarrass them? Are they afraid of failure? Do they not have the skills required? Or all of the above? Maybe it was because of a previous leader, or uncertainty about a new strategy. Regardless of why they feel uneasy, you cannot have them blocking progress. If they do not feel comfortable taking risks or are even terrified of doing so, you are the one who is going to hand them a life preserver to get out of the fear zone.

'Supportive risk taking
enables trust'

Change Agent #1

Before your first Model Team selection day, it is extremely important to articulate a burning platform to necessitate a major change folks will want to get behind. Convincing upper management of the need for support and investment does not have to be hard. Build your business case and be clear on the "why" (see Chapter 2 for structuring the case). Perhaps you have nowhere to go but up from a service delivery perspective. Maybe your customers are waiting far too long to get answers. Maybe your employees are leaving the company far too quickly after training. Or maybe your business unit is running over budgeted costs by more than 10%. If so, you are facing both a top and a bottom-line problem. When I have taken on transformations, in my initial 30-day assessments, I have almost always found a clear lack of trust and order in the teams. This is probably your biggest issue.

Taking on a big challenge as you enter a new role is exciting. It could possibly be making something work that a previous leader could not, which can make you both nervous and hopeful. You will have new ideas to make the operations turn out the way folks had planned, and perhaps even a bit better. I have seen leaders give up after just a few months when costs are spiraling in the wrong direction. But your leadership has brought you in to right the ship. You like these folks, and want to do a great job. You know they genuinely care for customers and employees. Your prior experience at Fortune top five companies, leading people through continuous improvement and customer focus, has always come in quite handy in these situations. Your experience will be put to the test. Your senior leadership wants to see big change fast. Luckily for you and me, we don't hesitate to do what we know needs to be done.

You might discover a perceived bureaucracy in your direct staff's mindset. Maybe it is also obviously present in several internal constituents. The team follows policies and procedures to a "T". They always ask for permission. There are clear policies and privacy guidelines that needed to be followed. You get all that. You just cannot understand the suppression of innovation. One of the first things you do upon your arrival is go to the frontline. You will watch and listen to the live interchange with customers. You will try not to disturb them. You will be engaged and curious. I hope you ask them, "Does this happen a lot? Any, ideas on what we could do to fix it?" The spark of energy coming out of the frontline will be electric. They are usually full of ideas: good ones.

Generating a Groundswell

I have always been inspired by employees' ideas. It helps me envision a goldmine of opportunity to fuel years of product innovation and productivity. I have experience in mobilizing teams in many different businesses. I have been on the Toyota production floor in Japan where I learned how to empower the frontline. I remembered what it felt like to witness a cable harness installer pull the rip cord and stop the entire Lexus SUV assembly line because they found a defect. I remembered the sweltering heat of summer in a Hitachi condenser plant, where I was learning how to organize people, machines, and material flow into manufacturing cells that churned out defect-free parts in a cool symphonic rhythm, every 45 seconds. I once conducted a green-field circuit board manufacturing plant start-up in Mexico. I learned to speak Spanish in six months so I could communicate with a frontline group that worked diligently and always sought ways to add value to the business. I translated all this manufacturing experience into running multi-million-dollar business processing teams. I love service and working with the frontline. My respect for employee empowerment integrated with business processes, _and_ profitability, has proven invaluable to me in the way I have chosen to lead others. Your respect for the intellect of the frontline will become your superpower, once you learn what to do with it.

Variation in processes and the treatment of employees can wreak havoc in an organization. When there are no standards to follow, or there are multiple standards in use, the workforce may be disillusioned in respect of its ability to change the situation. You might find some of the managers or supervisors are coasting along in what the authors Coffman and Sorensen of _Culture Eats Strategy For Lunch_ calls "ROAD Warrior status (Retired on Active Duty.)"[6] The book notes that "decades of organizational data suggest that approximately one out of every three employees currently works at the corner of Helpless and Victim." You have probably seen this yourself when you are not consulted about changes and they happen anyway, or you are unable to make a difference in the way your work is performed. Over time, if this is not remedied, you may become tired of it and check out mentally, though you can't check out physically due to insurance, mortgages, and the like. Ask anyone who doesn't trust their boss if they are engaged at work. Yeah, that's a big no there too.

It is not all the business unit leader's fault. It was no one's fault. Unfortunately, as I've seen with far too many companies and teams, the blame game can run rampant. Everyone wants to save their skin, so they keep throwing darts at each other. They fail to see that the enemy is on the outside, not the inside. In fact, on the inside are these beautiful people, like the supervisor who showed up with her galoshes and fishing pole. She was not giving up. She wanted a better way. She has probably been with the company for over a decade and has handled far too many customer escalations in her time. When we engage the frontline AND enable them to implement solutions we create a groundswell that turns into a tidal wave of self-directed change.

Choosing to Change

Right in front of you, this supervisor (let's call her Marie), is fighting for a better way for her customers, and for her team. You listen intently to her five-minute pitch and those of the other supervisors who shared their hopes and dreams. Your whole staff does.

Some of the supervisors will have prepared pretty PowerPoint presentations. Others may shiver in front of you with handwritten notecards mumbling their words. One leader might bring members of her team in on the deal and have them pitch parts of the presentation. They are all very creative and engaged. This is exciting to them. They are being noticed and asked to be part of the change. Until now, the change had mostly happened **to** them and not **with** them.

The leadership team and you will make your notes and tally your scores for each group. You will use a simple high-to-low scale (see appendix for template) to assess the supervisor's ability to:

1. Be Adaptive to Change

6

2. Understand Model Team Purpose
3. Deliver Results
4. Want to Succeed

At the end of the last presentation, you send everyone but the leadership team out of the conference room in order to deliberate on your choice. What happens next will give you great hope.

The team shares their notes about each presenter. One of your site business unit's leader's eyes are welling up when it comes to her turn. She begins choking up as she says, "I never knew Marie had that in her." She has been impressed by Marie's ability to articulate the unequivocal need to change and overcome a fear she harbored. At this point, the whole room gets a bit overwhelmed, but not with fear-with joy. Pure joy erupts as you all realize the team wants to move forward in making lasting change. This is half the battle and this hurdle has been crossed. Bingo.

'You win more when
folks choose to play'

You have decided Marie and her team will be chosen to become the first Model Team. They will embark on an intense six-week journey of training, instilling daily operating discipline, becoming transparent with their metrics, and change management, while still doing their regular day jobs. You cannot stop your 24x7 operations. You will have to find a way to figuratively "change the oil while the car is still running". And, up to this point, not a word has been said about any prize or recognition. It isn't necessary. They know the reward will be winning at delivering better employee and customer experiences from here on out. This was all the motivation they had needed to get jazzed up and put on the waders.

Fishing image: Freepik via Flaticon.com

Model Leader Reflection-Preparing for Transformation

1. What have you learned from listening to employees and customers?
2. What is your burning platform for transformational change?
3. What can you do to prepare yourself for a big change?
4. How can you help your team get ready to make the change?

Chapter 2

Transformational Leadership... Model Teams Bring Out the Best in Everyone

So, how many employees does it take to change a lightbulb? Well, that depends. This is always the answer any good *Six Sigma*[7] and/or *Lean* trained person would give when faced with a difficult question. There are so many variables one must consider when answering this question. For instance, how high up is the lightbulb which needs to be replaced? Is it a high-voltage situation? Is it a union environment? Is this an emergency? Who did it last time? Is it in the employee's job description? Aargh! Can we just change the lightbulb already?

This may seem a bit far-fetched, but I assure you, changes as simple as a lightbulb replacement can become stymied in corporate bureaucracy. The solution I have found works best is by simply asking the employees closest to the physical situation. They will probably tell you, "Just call John, or Suzy, or whoever did it last time." They will take care of it – as long as you let them. If there are too many policies, procedures, approvals, handoffs, or other baloney in the way, this lightbulb-changing issue can become a nightmare.

Maybe you have asked your employees about the lighting issue. They told you it is really easy to to make the change, but spending is frozen, the legal team will not approve it, the quality group needs to review alternatives, and the safety team needs to see the fall protection training module completed by

100% of folks in the department before anyone moves a muscle. You might have real customer issues burning up your email box and this plethora of red tape is just too much effort for too little reward. This could be true, but what if you are overlooking a more fundamental issue of how things get done in your team? What if you realize that this is not just about the lightbulb. It is indicative of a bigger problem such as the willing adoption of the new software platform, or working in the office regularly, or their need to get your input on nearly every single thing. Maybe, they just don't know what or how to change. You want to empower them, but you are not sure if the effort is worth it.

The Business Case for Model Teams

I have developed and delivered many business cases over the years. The language of business is finance, and thus numbers are the foundation of any worthy proposal. To make the case for Model Teams I equate value to the outcomes of the investments. The value of engaging and empowering our teams to identify and make positive outcomes is quantitative. For example, there is the direct opportunity cost of less customer complaints and/or more revenue from increased sales. There are also indirect costs such as employee turnover and lost productivity from too many meetings, distractions, and so on. On the investment side of the equation, you may need to fund a continuous improvement office to assist in the change (more on this in Chapter 3).

Here's how it might sound: "I propose we invest roughly $200,000 in developing our team to deliver greater operational performance which will in turn yield more than $1,000,000 in cost savings and revenue growth. This is a five to one return on investment in the first year. The team has already demonstrated great ideas for improvement and a willingness to learn. We will engage and empower them with continuous improvement training, disciplined operating mechanisms, visual metrics to track progress, and a prioritized innovation pipeline to bring the best solutions to life. Right now, it is costing us 15% more than it should for staff to respond to increased customer complaints, and an equal amount in lost productivity with everyone on calls to discuss simple things like changing lightbulbs. There is a better way to organize our efforts, harness the intellect of our employees, and empower them to deliver better customer service. I have a plan and I know we can do it."

Your investment cost and returns may differ from the example above, but don't be afraid to put it in writing and run it up the chain of command. Truthfully, I have heard "No, not right now," many times. However, when it comes to 1) investing inside the company, 2) providing a path to stable operations and 3) building up the bench strength of the group, I rarely met a rebuttal I couldn't refute. There were times when investments could not be afforded. Getting even one single person hired onto the team may not be in the cards. Eventually, you have to decide to change, or die. I had to get creative and re-purpose staff to the continuous improvement office and borrow resources for major change events to prove to myself and others there was a better way. When you are intent on leading your way out of something, don't take "No" for an answer.

As you prepare your business case remember this: Empowerment, or rather, enablement is key to productive workplaces. If you and your employees are enabled to make the change, then doing so becomes simple. One can be enough to change a lightbulb: one able-bodied, enabled employee who sees the problem, finds a solution, and executes it, simply because they can. If not, that light is out for far too long, people are in the dark, and you spend far too much time and money trying to fix it. As leaders, we can both overthink and underthink things, especially when we are in a business with multiple departments, metrics, and priorities. The reality is that our solutions to not only the lightbulb question, but also bigger ones such as how to grow revenue, increase profit, gain market share, etc., exist within the minds of those closest to the work. We just have to bring it out of them.

It's Not Just Business, It's Personal

I believe care and concern for employees are vital to the prosperity of all. Perhaps you remember reading about the Hawthorne Effect[8] where people in various studies changed their behavior, purely because they were being watched. The term was coined in 1958 by Henry A. Landsberger when he was analyzing earlier experiments from 1924–32 at the Hawthorne Works (a Western Electric factory outside Chicago). In the Hawthorne case, they had commissioned a study to see if workers would become more productive in higher or lower levels of light. Under certain conditions, the workers' productivity seemed to improve when changes were made, but then slump when the study ended. It was suggested that the productivity gain was a result of the motivational effect created when the researchers showed interest in the workers. Personally, I believe it was the care and concern shown to these workers, along with accountability that made their productivity higher.

> "People don't care how much you know until they know how much you care." – *Theodore Roosevelt*

I want to share a pivotal experience I will never forget. I knew something was wrong when I heard Maggie, a supervisor describing the reason for one of her employee's less than stellar performance. She said, "Jane has to work the overnight shift – you know, she is a single mom with five kids." I did not understand what Maggie was saying but could imagine why there might be some performance issues for Jane. Taking care of five kids all day and then working through the night must be grueling. I remember having a newborn and then going to work all day. I was exhausted due to a lack of sleep from the night feedings. I was flabbergasted by the supervisor's apparent callousness. My gut began to twist. I wanted to know the real reason Jane's performance was not up to par, so I asked Maggie, "What does that have to do with her job? I mean, it must be incredibly difficult to feed those children and ensure they have a safe place to live, especially on her salary. What training has she had in the last year? What does she aspire to do here?" It was at this point Maggie's eyes began to well up. She had never thought about Jane this way. She had never heard a leader care beyond the numbers. It was especially awkward because I was her boss's boss's boss. Three levels up. Having this kind of discussion about a frontline employee was a turning point for Maggie. It was a lightbulb moment for me to see how, when a supervisor starts to empathize with their employee's perspective, they take a big step towards a more caring and trusting relationship.

Great Leadership Requires Great Listening Skills

Here's another example of the power of listening to employees. Do you conduct regular employee town halls or discussion forums? If so, you know they are a great way to open lines of communication between the frontline and the leadership team. The next question is: do you conduct them with all shifts and locations? If you honestly have not, it could be helpful to imagine what might happen if you did. Let's picture one with your night-shift team. Unfortunately, these groups, like many who work outside of the normal 9-5 business hour shift, are often ignored, under-served, and under-represented, but absolutely necessary in order to run a 24x7 operation. There you are, at 4:30 a.m. with these folks. Sure enough, you and your leadership team are getting an earful. These employees probably harbor a bit of pent-up frustration. No one ever talks or listens to them. There is a lack of advancement training, no career path, and near zero recognition. They feel invisible and underappreciated. However, they know they are the only ones there to cover a critical shift. If it happens to be at a company in a first-responder or healthcare field, the work they do is often lifesaving. They know they are important. They wonder if you have even noticed.

You get to know the leader of this group. This supervisor is a hard-working woman who keeps the lights on as best she can and she has been there for many years. On the other hand, many in the team have become disillusioned that no one appreciated their value; a whopping 50%+ have left the company in their first year. The ones who stay need a paycheck, and some continue to hope a more enlightened day might come. That day is today. Your leadership team and you are listening to them. Finally.

'Seek to understand in order to be understood'

What they have told you opens new doors of opportunity for the business. Two of them speak up and say they have not had formal training in years. Most of what they know has come through osmosis or trial and error. The other heads nod in agreement. Next, they want to know a better way to deal with clients who abuse them because they are annoyed at being disturbed in the middle of the night for all kinds of matters, especially non-urgent ones. Their input turns into a beautiful idea, one of many more to come, about what clients value and what they don't. You find out your company is tagging all kinds of work as urgent, when, to the clients, it is not. You listen not only to your employees, but also to the supervisor who wants to be better able to care for her team. You are now reveling in the opportunity to improve your cost and service experiences.

The most amazing thing you find is that the team simply wants some appreciation. You ask what comes to mind. Can you believe what they ask for? Ice cream. They want an ice cream party as a special treat every once in a while. You deliver ice cream the following week in appreciation of their efforts and ideas. This is just one of many aha moments for you and your leadership team on the power of engaging with the frontline. The employee idea to update the handling of urgent requests saves the company millions in labor by reducing unnecessary work. What a win-win-win it is to eliminate a job the client didn't want in the first place, work the employee would probably get yelled at for doing, and time the company could spend on more value-added activities. There will be hundreds more ideas like this, yielding millions in additional revenue and cost savings. All of them are found by simply listening and engaging.

Employee Experience vs. Customer Experience

What we know from years of research, and simple common sense, is that the better employees feel when doing their job, the better their service to customers will be. Simply put, a great employee experience is directly correlated to a great customer experience. We know a great customer experience leads to better profit and growth. *The Effortless Experience*[9] by Matthew Dixon, Nick Toman, and Rick Delisi noted that 94% of customers who had a low-effort experience reported that they would repurchase from the company, while only 4% of customers experiencing high-effort interactions would. And 88% of customers with low-effort experiences reported an intent to increase spending with the company, compared to just 4% of customers with high-effort experiences. The level of effort in the customer's experience is a direct result of the people, processes, and technology of the company. The same people, process, and technology deal is exactly what the employee must experience every day too. I think of the relationship between the customer-employee experience and profit-growth in linear terms as expressed in Figure 1.

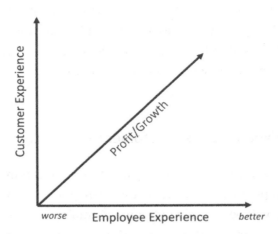

Figure 1–Profit as a Function of Employee and Customer Experience

As the employee experience deteriorates, what happens? Not only does the direct customer experience within the interaction worsen, but profits and growth decline. To prove the point, just consider attrition costs caused by a bad work environment. How much does it cost you to hire an employee? If you take that figure and multiply it by two or three because they leave in the first six months, you replace them, hire and train again, that one also leaves, and oh my. The dollars quickly start to add up.

Is it possible to have a great customer experience and a terrible employee experience? One might reference a company where we hear employees aren't happy, yet leaders tout their rising growth and profits. This is simply a fallacious argument. These companies could have much **better** profit and growth if they didn't churn through their employees so fast. Hiring, training, and disciplinary action take a lot of cash. For example, let's assume the cost of turnover per single low-wage hourly employee (~$15/hr) is $12,000. This figure may include recruiting, interviewing, onboarding administration, and initial training costs. If you are leading a team with 150 lower-wage employees, and your turnover is on average 30%, you are losing more than $500,000 every year to employee churn. This does not include the non-productive hiring and loss periods, nor the cost of customers lost because there was no one there to help them. That is just nuts.

Companies that focus on creating great customer experiences can naturally improve their employee experiences by engaging them in the design. We know higher customer effort experiences lead to higher costs to serve. Case in point, not having enough staff to answer customer service calls leads to salespeople fielding those calls. If the customer cannot reach a customer service rep, they call their salesperson. Not only is this a more expensive service interaction, but also the customer is not likely to be in the mood for buying when they are taking out their frustration on the sales team.

Jenny, who works in pharmaceutical sales, recently shared with me the enormous burden she and her customers feel due to the mandatory prior authorization processes required to obtain specialty drugs. The barrage of red tape cannot possibly come at a more difficult time for patients and their physicians. Just imagine what it is like to get a horrible diagnosis of rare blood cancer and hear there is a drug that could help. Your fear is amplified when you hear you do not qualify for treatment. This is not because of your pathology, but due to your insurance policies. The option to pay out of pocket is not even an option due to the quagmire of payer-payee processes. Your physician is at the mercy of Jenny and their administrative staff to try to work some magic and get the paperwork submitted and approved in time to save you. Jenny noted it can take weeks on end and is completely manual. Why does this experience have to be so onerous?

Taking a design approach to creating great customer experiences can help. Doing so requires performing *Customer Journey Mapping*, developing customer feedback systems, and the like. Your customer service team is a great asset for these exercises and they will be glad you asked. I have taken part in and led many such exercises. As a reference, I recommend *Chief Customer Officer*[10], by Jeanne Bliss as a guide to understanding and crafting your customer experience program. Her "guerrilla metrics" provide a concrete set of measurements you can use to formulate your Model Team dashboard too. I will expand on the formation of dashboards in Chapter 4.

> ***Customer Journey Mapping****: a tool used to outline a company's product and service experience from the clients' perspective that can also provide valuable insight to the employee experience*

Organizing for Success

So, you want good customer experiences, and now you know you need to create good employee experiences to achieve them. You might be thinking, take care of your employees and they will take care of your customers. Sound familiar? Probably, but how? How do you go about setting up the best environment for your employees? I had to face this question many times. When I started leading a call center that was the subject of an MIT case study[11] , first-year agent attrition was very high. The day I arrived, there was a crowd of people in the lobby being hired in. We didn't need the people because of growth, it was to replace those we had lost because they had walked out. The environment was not pleasant. Was it the pay, supervisor, benefits package, work, co-workers, customers, or the systems? The answer is, yes. The employee experience was an enterprise full of people, processes, and technology and it was not working effectively until we began to listen and realize what our employees were being asked to do.

A recent article in the Harvard Business Review titled, "Rethink Your Employee Value Proposition... Offer your people more than just flexibility,"[12] further articulates just how important and challenging, it is to attract and retain talent today. The authors highlight the way that pay and perks (including working remotely) are only part of the equation. Providing opportunities to develop and grow, creating a culture of belonging, and giving clear meaning and purpose to the work are equally, if not even more critical.

I have found a repeatable way to create an inspiring culture, development opportunities, and clarity of meaning in work for teams. It starts with one team, one Model Team, at a time.

What exactly is a Model Team? It is a small and scalable team you focus on to enable long-term operational success. It starts with a single team within your enterprise, say 5 to 30 employees led by a dedicated manager/supervisor, which you can shape into the kind of team you want others to become.

> **Prototype**: a version of a product or service created to prove viability in generating business value.

I had one business unit create three Model Teams in total. Then I moved to a different business where we created six because it was twice the size of the first and much more complex. Most recently, I transformed every call center supervisor group into Model Teams, over 40 in total. I never did it in cookie-cutter fashion, as we all know a rinse and repeat method does not work when we're talking about real people. It is truly about creating a prototype, then another, then another–a few or even just one small team at a time. By taking a step-wise approach you can quickly scale change across the organization. You focus on one team who demonstrates the way you want all of them to work. You don't wait for perfection. You progress until the team is good and stable enough for you to start another. Again, the premise is to build one team that can then be a model for the next to follow in terms of goals, learning, and engagement. As time goes on, the first Model Team will transform to the next level, and so on, and so on. The next Model Team will innovate on the standards of the first, but with a head-start. Change becomes a constant with adaptation and learning within and between the teams.

> **Model Team**: a 5-to-30 person team you train, organize, ideate with, and coach to enable long-term operational success. It is akin to "prototyping" an ideal team. Depending on the size of the organization, you could form one or several teams to scale business transformation. The teams learn to become self-directed leading to sustained superior performance.

For instance, after Marie has come to the conference room in her waders, you choose her to form a Model Team in order to prove to yourself and others that you can escape the chaos and operate more effectively. A couple of months after they are up and running, service levels are improving. Attrition is declining. Morale is up. Costs are declining. You have broken through to create a culture of empowerment, innovation, and having fun. You are looking for the next team to model on this one.

A Method for Change

Model Team Methodology™ is comprised of seven tollgates happening over the course of just a few months, as listed below. (Refer to figure 2 for a full cycle view.)

1. **Select** a Model Team
2. **Train** the Model Team
3. **Instill** Daily Operating Huddles
4. **Visualize** Metrics
5. **Innovate** with Employees Constantly
6. **Coach** Change Leadership
7. **Recognize, Reward, and Promote**

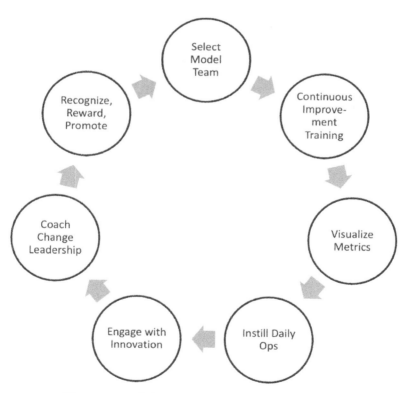

Figure 2–Model Team Methodology™ Lifecycle

Model Team Methodology™ helps you go about transformational change one step, and one team, at a time. It can be implemented with in-person, remote, and hybrid teams. Refer to Chapter 10 for more detail on leading virtually. While it involves several steps, it is not slow. You better get your giddy-up suspenders on to make big change happen. Once you decide it is time, don't look back. Go for it. Your team is counting on you. They need you to listen to them to keep your customers coming back. By committing to building Model Teams, you will become a better leader. If you're ready to swim, let's go find a pool.

Diving image: Perkasa via Flaticon.com

Chapter 3

Starting Out... Commit to Continuous Improvement

What's next and where do you start? You might be a real go-getter and head right to step one to select your team. However, let me give you a life preserver before you rush off. As a precursor to starting any major transformation, I recommend having a small Kaizen Promotion Office (KPO) in place. Some firms may have a single person, or they might utilize an existing program management office. Forming a Kaizen Promotion Office (KPO),[13] as many companies that want a pervasive continuous improvement culture do, is a must. It is even better if you can do so with a leader promoted from within the team.

The KPO should be small and have the sole purpose of training and coaching the teams in continuous improvement and change management. See Figure 3 below for an example of the organizational structure of a KPO. This size of office can typically serve between 500 and 1000 employees and multiple Model Teams depending on the mix of products and services. See Chapter 8 for more information on the ambassador role designed to supplement the KPO.

> **Kaizen Promotion Office (KPO)**: *a central group who manage projects, train employees, and facilitate change through continuous improvement techniques. The Japanese word "Kaizen" literally translated means "change- for good".*

If you are not familiar with Kaizen, it is a Japanese word meaning "Good Change". It is most commonly associated with the Lean practices founded by Taichi Ono and Toyota[14] and is known more widely as continuous improvement. I have been a Six Sigma black belt and continuous improvement practitioner for decades. What I know to be true about both Six Sigma and Lean is that they are logical, but not intuitive. You need to invest in the learning and guidance of these tools to have them work for you effectively. Ever since I was exposed to the techniques, I have been implementing these practices in my businesses because they deliver real results.

If your firm is not equipped with a KPO, you might consider hiring an expert. There are several great continuous improvement consultants out there including the Shingjitsu Corporation[15], with whom I have had the pleasure of working for many years. The investment you make in continuous improvement help will pay dividends for years and years.

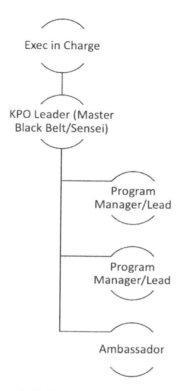

Figure 3 – Sample Kaizen Promotion Organization Structure

> **Six Sigma**: A set of problem-solving tools used in design and development of products and services, most commonly referred to in process management.
>
> **Lean**: a methodology used to engage people in continuous improvement – like Six Sigma but with more focus on the value delivered.

Model Leader Reflection–Creating a Model Team

1. Do you have a KPO in place? If not, what can you do to get one?
2. Do you have a group or two in mind who can vie to become your first Model Team via a "Shark Tank"-type session?
3. Have you consulted with your leadership team on the Model Team selection and development timing?
4. What can you do to adjust your calendar to allow you time to focus on creating a Model Team?

Chapter 4

Invest in Basic Training... a Little Investment for a Lifetime of Reward

In the fall of 1985, my mom drove me to Monterey, California to take the entrance exam to enroll in the electronic engineering program at DeVry Institute of Technology. My vision of where I was going was like the weather in this iconic part of the Pacific coast: foggy. I was not sure I wanted to go to college, or what to study. One of my high school math teachers had suggested I become an engineer. I thought, well, maybe this could get me a job as a roadie hooking up sound equipment for a rock band. I was young and impressionable. My father worked at Stanford's Linear Accelerator as a cryogen technician. He knew plenty of scientists and engineers, even Nobel Prize winners in nuclear physics. Dad's reaction was, "Yes, go do that." Luckily, I followed the advice and took the test to see if I could get into college. When I passed with flying colors, some of that fog lifted. I started to see a brighter horizon. I saw a future of adventure and learning. My mom was my biggest fan. She told me I could learn and do anything I wanted to.

I was very fortunate to finish college and begin my career at a company that made a significant investment in training its employees. They had enterprise-wide training for technical service, sales, and leadership. Their programs were and still are world-renowned. Right after I was hired, I went to their technical leadership academy to learn how to fix magnetic resonance equipment. It was a terrific experience, providing me with the ability to do what I had been hired for. Although I had an engineering degree, there was no way I would have survived without the investment in formal training. This company knew what they were doing. They always provided learning opportunities for their employees. From service to sales, all the way to executive leadership, they invested in their people. Occasionally they would outsource, but most of the training workforce was employed directly by the corporation. In addition to this, they provided a handsome tuition benefit to employees wanting to obtain external degrees. I achieved my MBA from Marquette University in part due to their generosity and belief in me. I suppose this is where my deep-rooted belief in educating the workforce comes from. I know the return on investment and have seen it pay dividends to many employees and the companies they work for.

A decade or so into my career, I was asked to teach transformational analysis as a part of a large Six Sigma program at the company. This was one of my hardest assignments ever. I prepared for the lesson by reviewing numerous exercises beforehand. I had performed my fair share of public speaking events and my stage fright was manageable. However, something about being in front of a class of really smart adults and having them stare at you with eyes suggesting they are thinking, "Does she know what she's talking about?" is terrifying. Training adults requires both technical and emotional skills.

What to Teach and Why

Why do you need to provide training? Not only does it make your team more competent and able to add value to the company, but also the prospect of professional development lights a fire of enthusiasm in your frontline. It enables them to come forward with smart questions and innovative solutions. And, let's not forget the business benefit of having a learning culture around you.

So, knowing why it's important, **how** do you go about training your employees, and, more importantly, **what** do you teach them? I hope you already have a new employee orientation program. It may be self-directed via an online course. That's fine. What about procedural things they need to do in their job? Maybe you pair them up with a colleague for job shadowing. That's fine too. It's not however the kind of training I want you to focus on.

One of the seven keys to creating a Model Team is providing continuous improvement training. However, don't panic about needing an entire education center to deploy your Model Team. You need to teach no more than basic continuous improvement skills to get rolling. The ones I have put into every frontline basic training plan are:

- **Eight types of waste** identification. This enables employees to recognize things in the workplace that do not add value to the customer. This in-cludes 1) defects, 2) inventory, 3) overproduction, 4) over-processing, 5) waiting, 6) motion, 7) transportation, and 8) downtime. Once employees learn what constitutes waste, they will be better able to offer ideas for improvement.
- **5S** is the process to sort, set in order, shine, standardize, and sustain a workplace. It is a great place to start teaching organization and order.
- **Process flow mapping** involves creating a visual outline of the sequential steps performed in delivering a product or service. This can be a simple block diagram with text boxes and directional arrows in between them to help people articulate and understand all the steps involved in delivering a product/service.
- **Problem definition** is the ability to define a problem using data and direct customer feedback. Understanding how to define a problem enables action that goes beyond a casual complaint to providing real improvement.
- **Measurement systems** provide a data-based way to track progress. Understanding what is measured, why, and how, is key to building business acumen. It is a must to enable self-directed dashboard reviews where the team is the one who keeps score of their progress.
- **Five-whys** is a troubleshooting tool used to find the root cause of problems by asking "Why", and continuing this process to the fifth level below the first obvious reason. For example let's take a simple issue such

29

as, 'Why is the printer out of paper? 1) No one filled the carrier tray. Why? 2) There is no paper to fill the tray nearby. Why? 3) The supplier hasn't delivered in over a week, Why? 4) We didn't place an order recently. Why? 5) Sue is off sick and she normally orders all the paper. Ah, maybe an ordering backup person, or auto fill program could help? This is especially powerful in moving thoughts and discussion beyond anecdotes to a deeper understanding of underlying systems and processes.

· **Seven-ways** is a technique used to illicit multiple options for solving a problem. It is performed using a draw it don't speak it method where each team member must individually sketch out seven possible solutions to a given problem. While I have seen teammates collaborate on generating the seven options, it is more effective when each team member first completes their sketches individually. This is harder than it may seem, but quite thought-provoking. Getting beyond two or three ideas can be tough, but it is better than having one or two people dominate the solutions which could unduly bias an outcome.

· **Try-storming** enables a team to move beyond talking about change to trying out various solutions to see which might work best. This is a technique and a philosophy designed to empower folks to try, fail, and try again. It is the action hero to brainstorming. It starts by taking one of the potential solutions and putting it to the test, not in real-production, or live service delivery, but in a safe test environment. Software engineers do this all the time. I have done it using real frontline people, processes, and technology in a conference room setting and/or an idle manufacturing cell.

· **Sustaining results** instructs people so they understand the metrics and rhythms to know what success looks like and feels like. It starts by understanding the metrics of a dashboard and why it is important to view the compilation of them as a set of data designed to fulfill customer, employee, and business goals holistically. They also learn the purpose and etiquette of operating mechanisms such as daily huddles and weekly team reviews to create reliable communication and problem-solving forums.

There are certainly more tools and techniques you could add to create a robust curriculum, but I know these will give your team a great foundation for becoming a Model Team. If you do not own these types of educational materials, the Lean Enterprise Institute[16] is a fantastic resource to call on. I have worked with them in the past and know them to be a credible and helpful partner.

'Understand why and
what you need to train'

Bite-Sized Nuggets are Easier to Digest

Where, when, and how you do the training, might be your biggest challenge. After all, you are running a business and this is another thing to put on top of your already full plate. You can call on your KPO (see Chapter 3 for more info on creating a KPO) to lead basic training. Maybe it is just a one-woman office, but get her on it. We are not going to teach anything she does not already know. As you gain ambassadors, which I will talk about in later chapters, the teaching tasks will become easier. If you believe your only choice is to outsource the training, ensure whoever you choose is going to be able to spoon-feed the team. Bite-size chunks of learning in a repetitive format are best. There is no single big-session learning that I have found to be effective when creating a Model Team. You need to use an active, hands-on, exercise-driven, reiterative learning plan that happens in short bursts throughout the working week.

As for when, don't let too much time pass once you have selected your Model Team. Ideally, the first training should be within two weeks. The sessions can be either in person, virtually, or a combination of the two. When do you interrupt production to perform the training? Do you need to go into overtime to get it done? If that's your only option, then yes. What you want is to interleave it through the normal workday by chunking it into itty bitty lesson plans of ten minutes or so.

Take into account the fact that what's made the social media channels so successful are small video snippets sharing before and after photos. Clips showing steps done out of order on purpose to get at the importance of sequencing work brilliantly. And most important, portray relatable content in the instruction by including actual employees and the business challenges they routinely face. Video instruction is one of the best approaches for auditory and visual learners, two of the main cognitive learning types. Because you want the entire Model Team to move forward at a similar pace, think through the delivery. If you teach the key points of your training through a video, do it as a group whenever possible. This accomplishes a couple of things. It brings the team together for a united purpose. It gets them all on the same page at the same time. And it provides everyone with equal opportunity. Encourage questions and seek to ensure understanding in the discussion afterward, a fundamental part of teaching.

Learn by Doing

Kinesthetic or hands-on learning is important too. For me, the best way to ensure understanding is by performing exercises. For example, you might try a scavenger hunt exercise to teach folks to identify seven types of waste. Let them roam mentally and physically through the workplace, identifying excess motion, overproduction, and the like. In one example, a simple solution to knowing what time it was in various parts of the world was found after training one of the teams to identify wasted motion. For a service desk team their motion was wasted in mouse and keyboard clicks searching the web to find out what time it was in Utah. What they found was that, instead of having to open a world clock on their desktop every time, they put up four clocks on the wall to reflect the Pacific, Mountain, Central, and Eastern Time Zones: cheap, simple, and highly effective. Note, this solution was innovated a bit later for all, with the launch of multiple time zone clocks on their desktop during boot up.

The Seven-ways tool I described is a great example of one that is best taught through a hands-on exercise. I am a huge fan of using the draw it don't speak it method for developing possible solutions. This one helps me at home with my husband too! Sometimes we don't get to all seven ways of how a renovation could turn out, but we get further than a shouting match when I start drawing out some of my ideas on paper. At work, it does wonders getting a team to innovate faster. Less talk. More action. It's really simple to do. Give each person a blank page and five to ten minutes to draw out seven different solutions to the proposed problem. The caricatures you get to see afterward can sometimes provide the deep laugh everyone needs to break up the fact that real change is about to happen. It can also bring out that one wild and crazy thought leading you to say, "Crazy, but it just might work."

For every Model Team you create, provide them with basic continuous improvement training. You can achieve concept learning in short 10-minute sessions. You can achieve learning that sticks using 15 to 30-minute "do it" exercise sessions. You can move to full-day boot camps in preparation for larger days-long change efforts. Whatever you do, start it, and keep it going. Teaching your team these basic tools can be done in a matter of two hours spread out across a few weeks. It's the practical application of the tools and how you and your leadership team respond to the events that will provide real learning.

Get Everyone Engaged in Learning

It is imperative to include the supervisors and managers every step of the way, even making them trainers when it is feasible. Motorola[17] learned the hard way that you cannot train employees who do not want to learn to work for leaders who don't want to make a change. They spent millions of dollars and hours educating their manufacturing frontline through the world-class MTEC and Motorola University. They learned early on "in the area of their plants where the workforce absorbed the whole curriculum of quality tools and process skills and where senior managers reinforced the training using new questions appropriate to the new methods... [there was] a $33 return for every dollar spent, including the cost of wages paid while people sat in class." For other teams who did the training, but didn't follow up, they either broke even or lost money. It is much easier to train in bite-sized nuggets and follow up with exercises as it gets digested more thoroughly by everyone, especially the leaders.

For the record, every session should be tracked through a learning management system, or a simple spreadsheet could suffice; just ensure you write down what and who you taught and when. You will undoubtedly look back on the records and be amazed by how much investment you have made. Consider these stats from Deloitte[18]:

> *"Organizations with a strong learning culture are 92% more likely to develop novel products and processes, 52% more productive, 56% more likely to be the first to market with their products and services, and 17% more profitable than their peers. Their engagement and retention rates are also 30–50% higher."*

I can tell you the statistics here are real. It is perhaps even more powerful if you choose to make a significant investment in employee training based on both customer and employee feedback. It shows you have heard them loud and clear, and it is something they want, so great! I applaud you for recognizing this. Perhaps, you see a need to raise the technical, clinical, and/or process acumen of the groups. You may have heard from employees and customers that they don't feel confident in their jobs, and you suspect a lack of ongoing training is a factor in your attrition rate. You might go so far as to ramp up your frontline employee training to provide, at minimum, 40 professional learning hours per year per employee. You should be bold and put it in writing as an annual goal for the entire team, to ensure it gets done. You know it won't be hard for the newbies to hit the goal, as new hire training is many weeks long. You are less confident about your tenured, and especially remote workers, for whom you know the process will be harder. There are only so many hours of company-required safety and compliance training one can take. Moreover, there is no way you are going to make the goal by taking the average of the total training hours over the entire team. You need to ensure this is an individual, person-by-person goal.

Your learning and development team will be busy searching to develop new training courses. Your employees will become aware that they are the ones responsible for creating and completing their training plans. Both of these things should make you optimistic about your decision to invest.

However, your leadership team needs a lot of discussions about what employees need to learn to fill up the 40-hour requirement. In hindsight, perhaps you decide that the quantity of learning goals is too arbitrary. Sure, it was a stake in the ground to gain traction in the learning organization direction. But, it isn't the quantity that is important. You realize setting the goal using quantity over quality could lead to some unscrupulous behavior to make the metrics look right.

The epiphany is the "what" and the "why" of the individual training programs. Having them guided by annual goals can mean taking a full year to realize your true learning needs. Thankfully when you engage everyone, especially your leadership team, you will be able to acknowledge any misses and change your trajectory. In doing so, you can reset your focus on foundational technical training. Maybe you will discover that basic networking terminology is a gap for your service team. Understanding how data gets from point A to point B is important. Proper technical vernacular is a confidence builder for them.

For sure, much of this is covered in new hire training, but now your team isn't following up as well as they could. Without these skills, every time an agent stumbles over the correct pronunciation of a networking parameter, the credibility of the entire company lies in question. It kind of feels like a duh moment to you, but the reality of the current versus desired competencies is stark. You think to yourself, your frontline joined this highly respected networking industry leader intending to become a part of the technical field. They get to interact with engineers, programmers, and data scientists. If they didn't have the basics when they came in the door, they expect your company will teach it to them.

You realize you have been assuming the team was providing enough learning during new hire training, but we know what happens when we make those kinds of assumptions. This awareness prompts you to enlist the intellect of those inside and outside your unit to help build content and teach. Another amazing thing happens when you do this. Your credibility inside the company increases. When you make a stand to say, "We don't know what we need to know. We need help to learn it," your peers step right up. Some of them even respond, "Me too... can my team join the training?" Have you simply found the courage to state the obvious? No, it isn't that heroic. It is more a humble recognition of the need to continue learning. With learning comes curiosity and confidence. And to think, it was an employee's idea that sparked the innovation to provide a new learning path to explore. The energy in the team perks up. None of this was easy, but nothing worth having is.

> *"We now accept the fact that learning is a lifelong process of keeping abreast of change. And the most pressing task is to teach people how to learn."- Peter Drucker*

Learning Through Experimentation

Trial and error is a great teacher. I have often heard, "You learn more from failure than you do from success." This is a core tenet of innovation and creating a Model Team. Every single team I have interacted with displayed some form of creativity and innovation. The degree and level of engagement varied with cultures. I have found it is highly dependent on the leader's ability to listen and encourage ideas to come forth. They also need to support risk-taking to allow the ideas, and team, to try, learn, and grow. You could reference the Try-storming technique I mentioned earlier in the chapter for help in doing this. Those companies I worked in where experimentation was encouraged displayed higher levels of success. Those who had consistent training plans and resources available excelled faster. Engaging your team in innovation that allows for trial and error is, well, more engaging.

Case in point, while working with an engineering team, we would issue "best failure" and "most likely to tank" awards. We would laugh and joke and celebrate the failed experiments. After all, how lucky were we to be able to learn from these exercises before they reached a customer? This group was a team of engineers who built multi-million dollar healthcare equipment requiring precision. You don't get to precision overnight. It takes development, which takes time, trial, and error. It was a culture of people who tried over and over again in order to develop great products.

One of my favorite lessons in learning about failure came during a large improvement project for a sister company's circuit board plant in Oregon. This traveling gig allowed me to advance my continuous improvement skills in a new environment. I was so excited to be given the opportunity. I remember arriving and opening the door of the rental car in the parking lot of the factory. I could distinctly smell the Pacific Coast pine trees. I took a deep breath of it all and felt so lucky to be there.

The company was investing in me and my whole job for the week was simply to learn. The event I was invited to was based on Kaizen. The Shingjitsu group was leading the teaching direction for the event with one of their very best Sensei (Master Coaches.)

We needed to restructure a manufacturing cell to achieve a single-piece flow because this is the best way to minimize waste and ensure each product is assembled with quality. A key part of the implementation was to install an andon system to visually alert maintenance and leadership personnel when the line was running (green light), and when it was down (red light).

On day three of this week-long event we were more than knee-deep in making change. A colleague and I tried wiring up the andon light and testing it out. Something shorted when we flipped the new andon switch on. Sparks flew. A few expletives burst from our lips, then we made a check to see if either of us was hurt. Thankfully, we were okay.

This incident had created a little commotion that drew the attention of our Sensei. He came over to see what was going on. My partner and I were sweating a bit wondering what the damage might be. As the Sensei approached, he was smiling. He started laughing and then said something extraordinary, via the translator. "Very good! You are making real change. Keep going."

My partner and I just looked at each other with expressions that said, "Holy moly! Really? This was good?" Then it turned to a grin. Now it was "Rock on! Let's blow more stuff up." We fixed the short circuit and learned to be comfortable taking risks forever after.

A couple of years later, I got the opportunity to work internationally, leading a circuit board plant start-up from a dirt floor warehouse. It was a really fun job. I was able to personally select the employees and institute Model Team practices from the start. It wasn't easy to make things the way my leadership team and I wanted them to be, even though we were starting from scratch.

There was trepidation and caution from other places the team had worked. There were cost and time pressures on all of us. The mothership factory back in the USA had its views on how it wanted things to be. I respected all of this and yet wanted to do something the home team had been unable to achieve. I wanted to create a single-piece flow in this factory to cut down on the waste and rework that can happen when multiple circuit boards are made in the same batch.

Have you ever been on a project spanning many months and requiring lots of trial and error? Regardless of the industry, perhaps you have gotten to a point where you have every step except for the last one figured out. Maybe your experience is a new design gig, or perhaps you are innovating an existing product. Getting the final piece of the puzzle to fit can be the most aggravating, yet satisfying step of them all.

For example, say you are working in manufacturing, producing multiple units at a time. The last part of the process requires just the right amount of manual adjustment. And, this means trial and error, every time. It might not be unusual to scrap eight or more units each time a new setup is required because they are done in batch mode with many of them moving through this step at the same time on the same jig. And, this could happen multiple times a week. You recognize this step is full of waste and thus money is constantly being lost in material and labor.

Now imagine your lead engineer is a gem: young, smart, personable, and hard-working. When you tell him you want to cut the jig that holds the units from carrying eight to carrying only one, he is hesitant. He might stop and reel back a bit, asking, "Boss, are you serious?" Here's your magic moment. You respond, "Yes, move forward." The jig you have instructed him to cut is more than a $40,000 dollar tool. Depending on the country you are in, this could be more than most folks' annual salary. It is a daunting proposition. He asks you several times if you are sure, and begs your assurance he will not get in trouble. You assure him it is okay to forge ahead. You give him your approval in front of the entire team. Cutting the jig is not just the responsibility of your lead engineer, but, a team decision backed by you, the leader.

What happens after this is eye-opening for all. The experiment might not work exactly as you all thought, but you get more ideas. The team makes another jig, and soon, you have a single-piece flow. You save hundreds of thousands of dollars by no longer sacrificing brand-new units while manually adjusting the last step. You have gained strength in your ability to try, learn, and make progress. I guess you could say that was one of your "burn the boats" moments. You have to risk the $40,000 jig to save ten times that. So in a way, it was a no-brainer, but it did take guts and determination.

'Be "okay" with failure
for the sake of learning'

Committing to Action

To empower your team in learning and experimentation, you first need to make sure you are empowering yourself. Yes, there is a chain of command, and we can't just proceed to spend company money without good reason and approval. You may even have self-doubt about the right way to proceed. One of the best ways to empower yourself and others is to commission Kaizen workouts.

Kaizen workouts utilize Six Sigma and Lean tools to enable a team to find solutions to problems, in a short period of time. It begins with defining the problem, envisioning a better future state, and chartering a small team to find a way to get there.

> **Kaizen workout:** bringing a team together to work on solving a problem in a short amount of time using Six Sigma and Lean tools. It typically lasts 1-5 days and is guided by a skilled facilitator. The team is empowered at the onset to make a positive change.

Take the case of Plumber's Supply Company[19] based in Louisville, KY. Their slogan says they offer "everything under the sun". Imagine the inventory and picking complexity this can create. Just two years after implementing Kaizen workouts, the 85-year-old company is realizing sustained financial improvement and a better customer and employee experience. "The company introduced Lean tools in an ongoing series of Kaizen workshops designed to train leaders on how to use the Lean tools effectively. They sought help from an independent Lean consultant who comes to help once a month. The management and frontline work side by side in the workouts with the guidance of the consultant. The first area where they applied the concepts and tools was—logically enough—the main point of customer value creation: the order picking process. Here, standardized work has reduced the time it takes new employees to learn all the storage locations and processes and become real contributors to the organization, from six months to three weeks. In addition, the changes halved the employee walking distance per day for packing and staging orders." As John Skees, Louisville's operation manager, states, "creating standardized work should be done alongside the employee you are trying to support and the focus should be on making their job easier." John says that Golden-Triangle thinking (also known as harmony between People, Process, and Technology) allows managers to create a standard that can be built into the work environment, so it is easier to do the work correctly than to do it incorrectly. "This provides a better-quality service to our customers and a better work environment for our employees," he adds."

As with many facets of life, a little bit of preparation goes a long way. Your level of preparation will make or break a Kaizen workout. It can take weeks to clarify the problem statement and set up the workout. In my experience most events start prepping at least six weeks ahead of the actual session. The data collection, team selection, and goal setting will empower and enable the team to find solutions with simulation in a few days. Once you set the stage, Kaizen workouts are a clever way of getting a bunch of people to help you get stuff done. Personally, I met people on a deeper level. I learned to facilitate ideation and debate. The biggest lesson was learning how to empower people–not just the ones involved in the problem-solving, but the leaders who we pitched to in the end. Once they were presented with a solution, by a team they had commissioned, they had to take action. That is empowerment 101.

Team Learning icon: Eucaly.p via Flaticon.com

Model Leader Reflection–Create an Engaging and Innovative Environment

1. How is the training of the continuous improvement tools with your Model Team going?
2. What do customers need changed, and how could you empower a Model Team to do it?
3. Is your response to question 2 a candidate for a Kaizen workout? If not, what ideas does the team have to make an improvement?
4. What could you communicate to cultivate a culture of learning with your team? (Hint: what are the wins and lessons learned so far?)

Chapter 5

Good Habits Lead to Great Results... Instilling Disciplined Operating Mechanisms

It was 8 pm on New Year's Eve 2005. My husband and I had enjoyed a nice dinner to look back on the year. We were headed home, as we had a big move coming up. I was changing jobs a week later, and we had to relocate again. I received a call on my cell.

"Hello, this is MaryAnn, how can I help you?" (I always answer as if I'm on service duty because I know no other way.)

"Hi, Ms. Camacho? It's Bob over here at the commercial contracting center. I'm just calling to let you know we've got everyone here and we'll be working through the night to get all the service contracts booked in time to make revenue cut-off before year-end."

"Well, that's wonderful, Bob. Thank you so much for your and the team's dedication to our customers and business. Happy New Year to you. We'll see you in a week when I get up there."

"You too Ms. Camacho. We're looking forward to having you as our leader. Happy New Year to you and your family." Click.

Then I turned to my husband. "I'm not sure about this new gig I just signed up for. The team is working through New Year's Eve to process service contracts. That is not my idea of a good time."

Don't get me wrong. I'm not averse to work. I work my tail off. I have been working since I was, well, forever. A strong work ethic is in my genes and upbringing. I grew up watching my father work four jobs at one time. He commuted 72 miles one way to work full-time at Stanford's Linear Accelerator, plus Navy Reserves, occasional nights running searchlights for store grand openings, and weekly farm-to-table sales of ranch eggs to his colleagues in the city. My mother put herself through trade school to land a great job at San Jose State University. I worked two jobs while going to school full-time. Yeah, yeah, so what? Everybody works hard, I get it. My beef is this; I despise waste and working in unnecessary crisis modes. I hate seeing people being pushed to the hilt when, in fact, with just a little preparation, waiting until the last minute to create a "rush-to-the-finish" crisis mentality could have been averted.

'You can smooth out constant crisis situations'

Imagine you are taking a new job, leading a service contracting center at a huge multi-billion dollar company. You might discover the team accepts contract submissions up until the very last minute of the financial cut-off. You wonder if one of the downstream effects of this practice is that salespeople are inevitably training customers to wait until the end to get the best deal. What if there were even more issues? Did the closing rush of the contract processes allow less-than-perfect paperwork? Had the salespeople learned to wait until the very end of the cycle in order to ease their workload? You wonder if anyone has thought about the burden on the processing team. By working this way, the field team will get the commission for getting that contract in, regardless of the timing. If so, while you know contract and deal timelines are not reliably predictable, this behavior is not cool. One group is taking advantage of another instead of them working in unison. You will clearly need to make some big changes to unify their efforts.

Start by Listening and Observing

In approaching the challenge of this new role, you will be drawing on what you have learned before: create a KPO, instill a culture of continuous improvement, and craft a few wins to get the team's confidence up. As the book, *Culture Eats Strategy for Lunch*[20] tells us, "We must learn how to: Ignite the passion in ourselves and our people. Connect our people to each other, our mission, and our purpose. Revitalize our cultures as a competitive advantage for our organizations, ourselves, and our families." You want the contract processing team to feel like winners, not a department that constantly gets dumped on. And, you want all the service contracts, and more, to get processed in a timely and high-quality way. Booking revenue properly is a big deal in sustaining a business. You will need to establish some discipline with clear operating rules, in order to have reliable service.

There could be dozens of employees in the team who process contracts and invoices for your business. Department tenure varies from 20 years to less than one. You notice the more experienced folks operate independently covering key accounts while the newer folks process routine work such as recurring monthly billing. It seems natural to you that the team is divided in this way. However, the newer folks want to be paid like the tenured folks and to have the freedom to manage their daily work. The tenured folks want no part of repeatable work, in order to maintain their craftsmen-like stature. You quickly realize the field commercial team loves the "craftsmen" as they constantly save the day and provide all kinds of favors from special customer reporting to booking a deal at the last minute before the close. All the work gets done, but there are clear silos and not much cross-functional flow of information.

As you arrive, you start your day by doing rounds to meet the team. You walk around and say good morning to everyone, stopping for a bit to introduce yourself and exchange pleasantries. You notice a few things on your rounds. There are huge stacks of paper. At some desks, they are nearly two feet high. On investigation, you discover they are service contracts that were either processed or waiting to be. "Which was which?" you wonder. How many were done, and how many needed to be booked and activated? No one in management knows. The piles dictate the workload, but there is no watermark to gauge where you are. In a few weeks, you hear a dreaded comment from a few sales reps in the field; they say they have nicknamed the service contracting center "the black hole." They have had the experience of sending paperwork in and never seeing it again. You aren't surprised, given the lack of organization you are witnessing.

The basics of continuous improvement teach us to look for the seven wastes. You can clearly see lots of contract inventory. They also teach us workplace organization using 5S methodology. There is no doubt that the stacks of paper need good sorting. You decide to employ these two basic techniques to start your transformation.

Assess and Create an Improvement Plan

First, you need to get a KPO in place as this is going to be a lot of work. Even though the work ahead is substantial, you will want to create a small team to facilitate (not do) all the work. Fortunately, Six Sigma and Lean practices are deeply embedded, or at least respected, in the culture at this firm. Many have been trained and are expected to use the tools in daily work. It won't be hard to convince upper management of the need to create a small team to lead your continuous improvement efforts. Nonetheless, you will build a business case to hold yourself and your team accountable for the investment and road ahead. You gather intel about the operations such as the number of contracts processed in a month, the number of invoices sent, the number of people, and wages. This gives you a baseline for your before and after vision. Goal-setting requires benchmarking, introspection, and pragmatism. It also takes guts. You set lofty goals to improve the turnaround time by increasing throughput by, say, 75%. You know there is plenty of idle time on your teams' hands. Yet, too often, there is also a crazy rush to the finish happening too often. You want to avoid these panic sessions and giddy up.

Your KPO might be formed with a proven leader from an adjacent part of the business who is a company-certified Six Sigma practitioner. This will be hire number one. You think hire number two should be a member of the existing team who possesses stellar credibility with the group. These two hires send key signals to the broader team. First, you require a high level of skills, and second, there is a way to teach improvement here. This move gives folks hope. Together with the two of them you become the trifecta of change management. But that isn't enough. You need the whole team to buy in.

Communicate and Execute with Discipline

You have become accustomed to regularly communicating via town hall-like sessions. You decide a good next step is to host one and share the state of the business and your initial thoughts about a go-forward plan. You might share your vision of what a better service contracting center and team could look like. You can also explain what it could mean for the company, such as more customers and a happier sales force. You can describe what it means for the team directly, like stable operations leading to fewer holidays in the office and better jobs. You know instituting a Model Team approach can make this happen, so you give all the employees an assignment. You ask who wants to form the first Model Team for service contracting. There will be some immediate interest in the group. There will also be trepidation. It's funny how, in almost all groups of people, there's a similar histogram of early adopters, followers, and nay-sayers. You will ask those who are interested to share their reasons why, in writing, with your KPO within the next couple of days.

You garnered interest from the town hall. The idea of a better working environment means that plenty of them are interested in taking part in the change. You and your leadership team decide on and set off with one small team of contracting specialists for your first Model Team. You will train them on the seven wastes and 5S. You ask them to help define daily operational metrics. You meet with them every day at the same time for a daily stand-up. You put a whiteboard up with the agreed metrics and denote the actual versus plan figures. You ask for their ideas and implement many of them. You have feedback sessions together with the field sales team to talk about results and what needs to change. You track every project and review them every week. You hold several week-long Kaizen sessions to work out solutions to gnarly problems. In the end, all this discipline over choosing a team, defining your metrics, listening to your employees, and acting on the best ideas culminates in one of the largest transformations the business has ever seen. The commercial operations team begins to walk a little taller. The swagger is coming back, but you must stay humble as you have a lot of work to do.

'Envision a before
and after picture'

Good Plans are Adaptable

Sometimes, the unexpected happens. As much as you may have planned, and been methodical about the transformation, imagine you get the call you didn't expect, nor want. Picture yourself a few weeks into your Model Team formation. You get a call from a Senior Vice President, who is supposed to be in Cabo enjoying the company's special annual winner's circle trip to recognize the best of the best in the commercial team. This isn't one of those, "Oh, dang we should have invited you here" calls. She had received a call from a very angry and important customer. They wanted to know why they had received a competitor's invoice that showed a different rate to what they were paying for what seemed like the same service. Uh-oh. How did this happen? You are likely in mild shock. What will you do?

All you can really do is investigate and provide an explanation. You might find out one of your most senior contract specialists had stuffed the wrong invoice into this customer's envelope. It was a perfectly human mistake, but one with grand repercussions.

Knowing how it had happened, you will still want to know why. Why was it possible for her to make this error? Could you turn to the 5-whys problem solving tool for help finding an answer? As I noted in chapter 3, the gist of the 5-whys technique is to ask why something failed or could fail, down to the fifth level. Most folks stop at the first level. They most commonly will provide remedial training and move on. Here is how you might go about it with the reason why statement, then your response:

- Level 1: "She should have been more careful," or "She has too much on her plate." OK, "Why is that the root problem?"
- Level 2: "She needs a better work environment, more space, less work, brighter light, and more coffee." OK, "Will that solve the issue?"
- Level 3: "Invoices are printed separately and then matched to a pile of envelopes." OK, "Interesting, why is that a contributing factor?"
- Level 4: "There is no quality assurance check before the invoice gets mailed." OK, "Would putting one in place prevent this error in the

future?"
- Level 5: "Not 100%, but if there is no downstream check, nor a change to the separation of invoices and envelopes to prevent a mix-up, then we risk having this happen again." OK, "Now we're getting somewhere."

Why did your client receive the wrong invoice? The systems and processes in place to send invoices to customers allowed it to happen. Even the most conscientious worker cannot be perfect every day. There was no error-proofing, no quality control, and no flow. Your experience has shown you mistake-proofing and flow need to be part of daily life, no matter if you are in a factory or a business processing center. At this point you might need to create another Model Team specifically for invoicing to deliver better results for your business, and customers.

'Know it's not the people at fault, it's the process'

Excellence Requires Discipline

There is a fine line between implementing disciplined operating mechanisms and providing too much oversight. Doing the latter leads to the dreaded micro management. This is why implementing Model Teams who are trained to be self-directed work so well. An excellence culture blossoms when a team learns how to lead itself. It is here that management transforms into leadership by allowing more time to focus on key priorities and the bigger picture.

You decide to follow the same outline as before. This time you hold a "Shark-Tank"-like review session. Interest in being a Model Team has grown among the ranks since your first foray. You choose a small invoicing team. Just as before, you train them, meet every morning via a brief stand-up, and choose metrics for the dashboard. You engage them in providing ideas for a new way of working to deliver quality output. You help them assess and implement the ideas for real change. You communicate the changes to everyone concerned before, during, and after they are made. The reward here is no more infernos. It won't happen overnight, but in a few months, the invoicing team will be delivering a much higher quality service to its customers.

When you want to make transformational change, you must set up disciplined operating mechanisms that you and your team can and will follow. The cadence, and frankly, repeatability in these mechanisms determines your team's level of cultural accountability. I remember standing in front of the big program board on a few mornings waiting for the review to start. Patience is NOT my strong suit. But, I stood, and I waited. I was doing this every week for weeks on end, and in the end, coaching for the timeliness, engagement, and results made for great outcomes. As they say in sports, winning happens at the gym, during practice, practice, and practice.

From my time running manufacturing processes, with team stand-ups every single day on every single shift, to improving boundaries for a back-office team, I have found it impossible to run effective operations without setting daily, weekly, monthly, and annual reviews. I made it a tradition at the end of every year to review my operating calendar, refresh it, and provide it to the team as we started the New Year together. I also provided my administrator with a yearly family calendar with key dates for vacations, school, and other predictable activities to make planning easier.

To this day, the period between Christmas and the start of the New Year has become a point of reflection for me. It can take a few hours to a full day for me to review and define the year previous and coming years. I don't do this to set absolute resolutions, but to give myself the gift of time for mental clarity. I have come to know myself better in these periods. It also really helps to put a framework for achieving success in place. I encourage you to give yourself the gift of reflection time in order to envision your desired future.

While even the best-laid plans can fall to happenstance, and spontaneity can be fun, leading your team requires clarity about where you're going, when you're leaving, and what you're taking on the journey. How you get there will certainly morph as you roll along.

> *"There is no shortcut to achievement. Life requires thorough preparation*
> *– veneer isn't worth anything." –*
> George Washington Carver

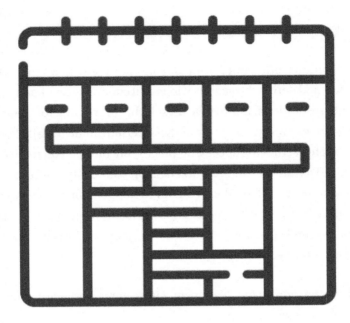

Planner Image: Freepik via Flaticon.com

Model Leader Reflection–Making Change Happen

1. What have you heard while observing live interactions?
2. Have you envisioned a before and after picture for the team?
3. Have you communicated this vision?
4. What measures do you have in place to track progress?
5. What can you do to engage in more *effective* daily, weekly, and monthly operating mechanisms?

Chapter 6

Keep Your Eye on the Prize... Visualize What Great Looks Like and Put it on a Dashboard

As leaders, we know to set goals, distribute them, achieve them, surpass them, and outright crush them. We rely on goals to tell us where we are going and how we are performing. But, what are our goals based on? Is it obligatory sales growth, positive margin accretion, and positive cash flow? At a macro level, yes, those are a few good signals of a healthy business. They are also end-game goals. To run a business, we need to understand the means to the ends. Even if you are not the one setting the company's high-level goals, I have yet to meet a CEO who wasn't ecstatic about seeing her staff flow them down and make them their own.

Whether I was setting or adapting strategic goals and executable priorities, I favored using the Hoshin Kanri method to do so. This technique is also referred to as "Policy Deployment" in Toyota Production Systems[21]. It is a method for ensuring that a company's strategic goals are set AND they drive action at every level within that company. Hoshin Kanri, when used properly, eliminates the waste that comes from inconsistent direction and poor communication. I find it a clear method to ensure work delivers results the company wants.

It starts with establishing a vision, then identifying three to five key strategic multi-year objectives. These are then meticulously broken down into sub-tasks for annual goals. What gets measured gets done and, as such, disciplined reviews are critical to the Hoshin Kanri process. Goals must be descriptive, specific, actionable, and timely, and then reviewed on a regular cadence. To identify relevant and timely measures for the sub-tasks, I find it beneficial to identify key moments of value creation and waste in a business process. Sometimes value stream mapping can be used, but even simple process mapping can help. While it might be straightforward to count the widgets produced and sold, identifying the trip hazards to doing so a far better sub-task to track. These hazards are waste and can easily derail us. Identifying waste is the harder thing for many folks to do.

> **Hoshin Kanri**: a method to set, communicate, track, and deliver a strategic plan within an organization. Derived from the Toyota Production Systems "Policy Deployment" method, it ensures a clear top-level vision is actionable via strategic multi-year objectives. These are then distilled into annual executable goals. Regular operating mechanisms to review progress using relevant and time measures bring accountability with results.

Waste Stinks

Are you one of those people who can smell wasteful work from across the room? Or, do you stumble over it like junk mail arriving in your mailbox? It takes a trained palette to see waste, or what the Japanese call "Muda" at work.

In a well-known automaker production facility in Japan, any associate can stop the line in its tracks to prevent waste. Everyone is trained to know it, see it, and take action to prevent it. I saw this type of system firsthand in multiple factories around the world. It is not always intuitive, but it is logical. Once you and your team are trained, it will be easier to learn how to spot waste and the opportunities that follow. Identifying this waste is imperative in choosing metrics to run your business because waste leads to mistakes and wasted money.

Where there is a high probability and/or risk of waste, metrics allow us the opportunity to act before it is too late. Whether you are in an engineering, manufacturing, or transactional operation, waste is waste. Holding excess inventory, over-producing, over-processing, unnecessary movement or transportation, waiting, rework, and defective products or services are all cash burners.

The hypothetical experience from Chapter 5 about the invoice sent to the wrong customer highlighted a big operational deficiency. A major part of the issue was probably a lack of relevant operational metrics. The team's goals were probably more focused on growth (the dollar value of new contracts booked) and cash (days until invoices were paid). Was anyone measuring the running of this invoice operations team properly before the dreaded call came in?

When we begin investigating any big debacle such as this, we find over-processing, waiting, rework, and unfortunately a defective service product. The employee who creates the defective product is probably working in batch mode, generating a stack of products all at once. Then, after the products are made, they move on to packaging. This is where the waste starts in the form of "overproduction".

Getting the concept of wasteful batch processing understood by an entire team is not a slam dunk. Hindsight teaches us that one big stack of invoices, and a big pile of envelopes, if not matched together perfectly, could indeed cause a costly mistake. Especially if they are sorted and stuffed manually. For example, you might hear some representatives say, "It's easier for me mentally to do all my invoice work, then put them in the envelopes, then walk them to the mailroom. I save steps and time this way. They could also say, "It's easier for my brain to focus on one process, as opposed to the whole stream of work for each customer."

They employees will make some good points. It can be easier to focus on one task at a time. However, having one person manage the entire flow is risky. What if they are absent? What if they work a little slower or faster than others? What if they make a mistake? What if there are changes made after the products are produced? The risk to the business and customers is so high. In the invoicing example, sending the wrong customer invoice to a multi-million dollar account, in the middle of a new contract negotiation, potentially risked several hundred thousand dollars. What if there was another way? What if we could visualize the process and institute metrics to reduce waste and increase quality?

Hands-on Visualization

To teach a team how wasteful any current process is, help them understand batch processing versus single-piece flow in a hands-on exercise. This one is super quick at ten minutes or less and perfect for an in-person micro-training session. Gather a few employees around a conference table and provide them each with a blank piece of paper and a pencil. They might all know each other, but ask them to introduce themselves as an icebreaker.

Part one of the training exercise goes like this:
1) Instruct them to write the first and last name of each person at the table onto the piece of paper in list form, starting with themselves, then the person to their left, and so on. When they are done, they signal this by laying their pencil down.
2) Set a timer and say, "Go."
3) When the last pencil is down, stop the timer and note the duration out loud.
4) Begin a quality control check asking each to pass their page to their colleague on their left. Instruct them to check their own name on their

neighbor's work for accuracy, finding out if their colleague had spelled their name right.

This is a bit of a comedic exercise for sure. Big surprise – there will probably be errors, or at least illegible handwriting! It will probably take thirty to ninety seconds to complete. You can all have a good laugh and then move on to the next part of the learning.

Part two of the training exercise:

5) Give everyone another fresh piece of paper. This time, ask them to write only their first and last name on the top of the page, then pass it to their neighbor.

6) Set a timer and say, "Go."

6) The next person writes their name, then passes the sheet, and so on, until all sheets are done and pencils are down.

7) Stop the timer and note the duration out loud.

8) Begin a quality control check asking each to pass their page to their colleague on their left.

Amazingly, you will probably find part two (a single piece flow method) finishes quicker, upwards of 30% faster than the batch process. AND there are probably no errors. Maybe you still have some illegible handwriting, but guess what? Everyone knows how to spell their name. The learning here is that, even when someone thinks they know it all, and can do it faster than others, doing one part of the process well, and engaging teammates to do the same for their part will yield better results. This exercise can be followed up with classroom training on flow versus batch processing including process diagramming via video instruction.

'Hands-on learning is more engaging'

Understanding how your operation moves from one stage to another in delivering products and services to your customers is the key to visualizing and choosing the right metrics with which to run your business. A great practice I utilize is to follow the sales/service ticket from start to finish. It is as explicit as it sounds. Find the place in your business where inception with a client starts and then track each step until the end. I highly recommend you do this if you have not already. It is an enlightening customer and employee experience.

After the single-piece flow training, you could begin a current process visualization exercise. To get a feel for what this is like, picture yourself back in the contract processing center. You have a hybrid office set up in a four-person style cubicle array with multiple groups like this. You have some reps working remotely too. Those who are in the office have their back facing the center of the array when they are hard at work on their computers and phones. You do not regularly see the ones working from home at all. We'll talk about this in a later chapter.

In the physical space, I have found the outer side of the quad cubicle walls to be a nice blank canvas on which we can picture the flow of a process. You too want to "see" all the steps, so you decide to engage your KPO leader, supervisor, and a few of the reps. You gather up the team, get some blank paper, pens, and pins, and move to the hallway side of the cubicles. No fancy software program or other tools are needed at this juncture. You will need to remain very basic.

To start the exercise your interchange with the team might go like this:

"What is the first step in the process of creating a service invoice?"

"Gathering all the changes, debits, and credits to the account for the month," says the supervisor.

"Good. Write that down on your piece of paper and pin it to the cube wall on the left side. We'll call that step 1. Now, what is the last step in the process?"

"Taking it to the mailroom," says one of the reps.

"Good. Write that down on your piece of paper and pin it to the cube wall way over there on the right side, like 20 feet down from the first step," you say.

This is fun as you are watching their eyes and body language saying, "What, way over there, really?"

You press on. "Now, everyone stand back and think for a minute. What comes right before taking it to the mailroom?"

"She puts it in the envelope," says the supervisor.

"Good. Write that down and pin it to the cube wall way over there on the right side, just before the last step," Okay, now, what is the step right before she puts it in the envelope?"

"I print it out," says the rep.

"Hmmm. Is that the step right before putting it in the envelope? Is there any checking for accuracy done before this?" you ask (smiling I'm sure.)

"Yes, of course, it goes without saying they check their work before they do that," chimed in the supervisor.

"Tell me more about the accuracy check,"

"Well, I make sure the print quality is OK for starters," said the rep.

"Okay, write that down and put it on the wall before the second to last step under the heading Accuracy Check. What else do you check for?"

"I check all the pages printed, you know; if there are ten pages, then I count them to make sure they are all there," said the rep.

"Okay, write down page counting, and put it on the wall before the second to last step under the heading Accuracy Check. What else do you check for?"

By the time you are done with this exercise, about two hours later, you have moved the first step to the left of the cubicle wall twelve feet. There are probably over 30 steps that go into creating and sending a monthly invoice to customers. The kicker that you and the team discover is that not all invoice creation follows the same process. You will begin to document multiple ways the different reps perform their work. One representative could be responsible for dozens of accounts using incredibly manual and varied processes every single month.

You want everyone to stand up for the entire process of flow diagramming. It moves quicker this way, even though it was and is time-consuming. Not everyone agrees at first, but getting all the process steps posted on the wall helps folks feel validated. Their voices will have been heard. This is a fundamental must-have in team dynamics. It's critical in Model Teams. The trick is not allowing anyone who is more vocal than others to dominate, nor to let them just talk. They must WRITE IT DOWN. Everyone plays here. Even the quiet ones who could not articulate the steps would help us put them in order. I have seen process flow diagrams span over 100 feet with paper and handwritten notes all over them. The sticky notes to highlight the waste will be your next step. At this stage, you already got folks talking and the existing operational metrics are probably feeling a wee bit inadequate.

'Stand (don't sit) for shorter and more effective meetings'

Going with "Good Enough"

The next part of your exercise will be to identify where the most failures occur in the process. You can rely on the Seven Wastes method to spur the identification. For example, the overproduction of multiple copies of the same customer invoices may be noted. There is probably a lot of waiting for the reconciliation of changes from accounts payable. Over-processing could happen due to changes from the field team coming in during the invoice creation time. Production of defective invoices might happen due to a lack of good processes. It isn't the rep's fault. It is becoming clear you need to change. You have just visualized how screwed up the current state is, and no one is going to settle for leaving it this way.

With a good current process flow in hand and a bundle of opportunities to identify it better on Post-it notes, the Model Team can go to work to set up a new flow line for invoicing. First, you lay it out on paper. Some folks will want to continue mapping the future state process until they get it just right. Nope. You will have to move forward with a "good enough" version. Undoubtedly, you will have a better process than before. Also, you are making this transformation in the middle of having to do real work. You cannot just stop and wait. Invoices still need to get out the door. Moreover, delays are usually simply an anti-change tactic.

Although you may get a lot of strange looks from folks, you want to really visualize the flow of work. Perhaps you could align lateral filing cabinets in a row through the center of the cubicle array and set up letter trays to hold the work in process. Yeah, it's on the computers, but <u>physically</u> visualizing the work, makes a huge difference. You print key steps on different colors of paper. You separate accounts payable reconciliation work from the ready for quality assurance work. Unfortunately, you have to print a lot of paper. Before this, most of the work was done on computers, but it is hard to see. And, when it was printed, it was put into stacks on someone's desk. You deliberately want the team to make the work visible, to see what was happening and where things were at for each customer and every step. It will feel like overkill. This is hard. Nobody wants to slow down the process by printing everything. The KPO leader and you need to remain steadfast as it is necessary to demonstrate where the batch-based defects are occurring. It is also necessary to enable the team to see what each other is doing. They may have thought they knew before, but there is much to learn. There will be multiple aha moments as you start flowing invoices one step at a time through the Model Team. Be sure to measure the time, quantity, and defects of every unit through every step.

'Visualizing workflow illuminates reality'

This Model Team may not be the first nor the last in this department. Another team will want to get in on the action. They learn from others before them and thus have a head-start and focus on creating flow. A big revelation for this group will be how much rework is occurring during multiple parts of the processing. You may have noticed in your walkabouts and team idea submissions that the contracts are being submitted with critical pieces missing by the field sales reps. Your processing team now decides to understand what is required upon submission. You help them create a checklist of key components required to clarify what is needed to improve quality and the completion rate. This move may not make your commercial team happy at first. There will be a mountain of change management required as everyone has their own beliefs and experiential knowledge. In order to rectify a high level of defects seen at the contract submission point, the processing team might decide to attach a highly noticeable "card" to a contract if it was missing "must have" components such as a "signature" from both parties, or "all" the attachments.

You find it funny that the process gets nicknamed "carded", and yet, your contracting rep empowerment vibe catches wind. This team has been able to change the game from a repair house to a revenue-booking machine. No more pushing incomplete contracts down the line and expecting someone else to fix them. These reps are now empowered to speak up, say what was wrong, and request a fix, by the deadline, or no contract will be booked. It might mean delays in commission, and revenue, if the defects are not resolved in time for a financial cut-off. You are savvy and know this is a forcing function for yourself and everyone else to get submissions right and not pass costly defects down the line.

Folks will soon figure out the new methods. And it will make everyone better. It certainly helps your company file faster, more cleanly, and compliantly. Because you measure the work at every key point from contract submission to obtaining payment for invoices, you now have excellent operational controls. You probably simplify the measures over time, but you will never lose focus on managing the total process by looking at quantity, time, and defects. You and your team feel so much more in control and that feels great.

Keep it Simple

A few years back I became the GM of field service operations for a Fortune Five Healthcare company. I was doing one of our weekly continuous improvement project reviews. One of the proposed projects was to create a composite service dashboard of key measures. The business leaders wanted a barometer of progress and a fair warning system for the customer, the business, and any employee issues. To the VP of Service and Quality, and the other GMs, the number of metrics they had to consider was huge. Some were daily, others weekly, and many monthly and even quarterly due to the nature of the data and reporting methods available.

Do you ever wonder if having umpteen different measures is truly necessary to run your operations? Perhaps it feels like an awful lot of tracking, analyzing, and little translating into action. What if your VP of Service tells you quite directly: "Yes, there are this many metrics AND probably more when you're running a business this expansive and complicated." Maybe you could challenge his response by asking, "Isn't less actually more?" You might not succeed in convincing anyone to track less right away. It will happen naturally. The scorecard will be too big to keep updated regularly. Some components will always be missing, or out of sync with the rest of the data from a timing perspective. It can be too complicated to understand the definition and gauges of each metric without having to explain them over and over. It might just get to the point where you are spending more time talking about the gauge of the measure than the actual data and what to do about it. Hopefully, over time your dashboard will be reduced to fewer metrics, automated, and made available on demand. It is a good lesson to accept the fact that "good enough" is okay when it is being accompanied by iteration.

Whenever possible, it is best to keep in mind the fact that less is more. There is a simple principle I return to when I am thinking about what to measure – K.I.S.S. – Keep-It-Simple-Stupid. The 4 Disciplines of Execution[22] and many other books emphatically tell us to determine our big rocks first. Keep those to the vital few: seriously, just one to three big goals maximum. From there, you can flow down to key performance indicators (KPIs) of both leading and lagging types. When we keep it simple, especially while starting out, we don't have to worry as much about updating the format of the dashboard. KPIs can and do change in response to end goals as well as identified waste traps. Despite the best-laid plans, the leading and lagging indicators may be in flux for a while until you get into a rhythm. It is more important to have the right measures than it is to have a cleanly formatted dashboard from the start. This data will drive your decisions and actions. Stay focused on that. Remember, what gets measured gets done. In the Weight Watchers® program[23], participants track their food intake against a daily points allotment. This very simple, yet disciplined act of tracking what one eats, makes a profound difference in the success of so many people. It is the number one determinant of successful weight management.

> ***Key Performance Indicators (KPIs)****: the vital few measures used to track successful business operations. They are derived by understanding the end goals of an organization and working backward to identify the keys to achieving them. For example, if employee satisfaction is an end goal, employee attrition is a good KPI to measure and analyze.*

I have found the sweet spot of managing operations is to have a dozen or fewer key metrics. Otherwise, it just gets too time-consuming and convoluted. Somewhere between the flow down of key measures and the bottom-up approach I described with the service contracting team example, you will find your vital few KPIs. Keep them in front of you and be ready to adapt when needed.

'What gets measured gets done'

Building an Operations Dashboard

Once you have your main goals and KPIs decided, it's time to put them on a dashboard. I have seen and used all kinds of methods, including printed pages taped to a wall, dry-erase boards, published web pages, and big-screen TV projection in a command center setup. I've even seen hospitals post their emergency room wait time in minutes on a highway billboard for everyone to see – now that drives a kind of operational excellence mentality, doesn't it? The method you choose depends on your work style configuration. If you have a remote team, an online dashboard, or at least the ability to cut and paste to a portable document is a must. One group used a shared drive and a spreadsheet. Another used a Microsoft Access™ database to produce a dashboard for teams working from home and other locations.

Dashboards can benefit a wide range of constituents. In a case study by HBR[24], Honeywell's Project Management team improved their agile development, capital allocation and scope changes through better dashboard tools. Facing multiple gyrations of spending requests, and project delays, they outlined a method to "provide timely and easy to understand numeric and visual reports of KPIs corresponding to project activities offering stakeholders a high-level view of essential metrics that show them the state of project performance." Their data and analytics team did so by understanding their user's needs, creating simple data views, making the interface user-friendly, and providing user support. This was key to enabling project managers to predict budget forecasts and ongoing performance more accurately. Similar to the visualization exercise our contracting team performed, starting with the end user's needs allowed them to transform activity into data, then analysis, then actions delivering better outcomes as a result.

Engaging end users in developing and revising dashboards makes a big difference. It is part of the learning and ownership process. We can achieve this with a process map exercise or at least start with key measures that are important to our customers. If customer satisfaction is important, start there. Know your percentage of customer satisfaction, net promoter score, or number of likes, or whatever numerical measure you require to monitor the progress of your company's success at delighting clients. It may take a few weeks, a few months, or even a year to flush out the right set of KPIs and dashboards. This is another reason I like the Model Team methods. You can start small and focused, and iterate as you scale. Once you feel confident in your dashboards, work to migrate to business intelligence tools to automate the data feeds and provide a more seamless user experience.

Putting a Dashboard to Good Use

Where and when you *update* the data, as well as where and when you *review* it are very important. Have a known date and time with repeatability when it is updated and published. Ensure the necessary reviewers, for instance, your supervisors, managers, and/or KPO team have access to it. Give them time to do this. You don't want to be publishing data at 5 p.m. for a review the next day at 8 a.m. Folks need time to digest and analyze data. With the help of business intelligence tools, you can integrate simple elements like trending and variation analysis to make this easier for your team. I have found success in having data finalized and published at least a day before weekly reviews, and three days before monthly ones.

Latent data is inherently past the time when it could be acted upon, but that doesn't make it useless. I have learned daily and even hourly metrics are necessary when you are running fast-paced operations. Think about whether, in the context of your customers, and operating mechanisms, there is a benefit. If you do not have a daily measurement available, find a proxy, or a leading indicator, and measure this every single day. It might take a while to get in the habit of tracking daily. It may even seem like overkill to be so deep into the operational details.

Weekly reviews provide a nice cadence for running continuous improvement and innovation programs at a senior leadership level. I also highly recommend you be inclusive in these reviews. Bring in the frontline employees with the supervisors and managers. Let them get a feel and taste of what it is like to look at the whole business in a single hourly review. Allow them the opportunity to present their ideas, lessons learned, and accomplishments. Nothing brought a smile to my face more than seeing a frontline rep smile from ear to ear just because of being invited to a seat at the table, and then observing them fully comprehend the "why" behind the metrics.

The cadence and rigor need to be predictable: the same time, every day, and every week, without fail. Whether in person or remotely, the projects must move forward. The places where we can see all projects at a glance aren't monuments. They are live work areas. You always want to be able to openly show both internal and external clients these work areas during tours. It provides transparency and authenticity to the teamwork. In hindsight, it is so much easier to prepare for reviews using this method of working. I will take a whiteboard over a PowerPoint presentation every day of the week.

How do we know when our dashboard is working? When we see the end goals tracking in unison with the key performance indicators. Professors Nicholas Bloom, Raffaella Sadun, and John Van Reenen performed a study with more than 12,000 interviews at companies in over 30 countries to learn about achieving lasting productivity relative to employing modern management techniques. Professor Raffaella Sadun explained the key finding: "If you look at our data, it's obvious that core management practices can't be taken for granted. There are enormous differences in how well managers execute even basic tasks like setting targets and tracking performance. And these differences matter: better-managed firms are at a long-term advantage; they are more productive, more profitable, and they grow at a faster pace."[25]

If you are detail averse, I get you. I prefer working on the strategic side of operations. However, I know that, if you want to deliver great results, you must inspect what you expect. This means setting a strategy and operational excellence. A dashboard is right there with your windshield and ignition. Drive on!

Dashboard Image: Eucalyp via Flaticon.com

Model Leader Reflection–Building an Operational Dashboard

1. Have you set goals?
2. What measures do you have in place to track progress?
3. Have you visualized your processes to see where both value and waste are created?
4. Do you have a simple dashboard working for you?
5. Do you know where you are in the pursuit of delighting your customers?
6. Are you measuring your employee's experiences?

Chapter 7

Harvesting Innovation... An Endless Supply of Ideas is on the Frontline Next to the Customer

Just a few months ago, I was waiting in a hallway outside a CT imaging suite in a prominent hospital. I was there with my father, who was getting scanned in preparation for a heart valve replacement. With nothing else to do but worry if he was going to make it to the procedure, I was innocently watching people come and go. Two staff members had walked in and casually greeted each other.

"Whatcha' been up to?" asks the first.

The second responded, "Oh, I'm over here doing this job for four hours a day. I don't know *why* though. I am really bored. I told the boss it was a waste of money to have me there. It would be better if they consolidated with the other location around the corner. I'll keep doing what they tell me, but I am the type of person who likes to work, ya' know?"

I am still sitting there, listening while trying to look like I wasn't. I couldn't help but be interested. This is a casual employee conversation ripe with opportunity. Maybe there's a deeper reason for the lack of clientele at the second person's work location. Maybe it was a slow day. However, what if it was a real business problem? What if this employee had a solution? I wondered if anyone would care to ask.

Respect Their Intellect

According to an article in Forbes[26] in a survey from Gallup, "highly engaged teams show 21% greater profitability." No kidding... it seems obvious doesn't it? But, what does engaging them mean, and how do you go about it in real work?

One of the keys I have found to engaging the teams I have led is to respect their intellect. Respect starts with asking questions. Engage them in feeding ideas and solutions to the business challenges you are facing. Regretfully, it took me a while to figure this out. In my earlier career, I wanted to be the one with the answers. I needed to be the smart one to feed my ego. One day, I woke up and realized I didn't want to be that kind of manager ever again. I saw myself acting like someone I didn't want to be. I'm grateful I had this revelation.

In his book, *Better, Simpler, Strategy*[27], Professor Felix Oberholzer-Gee referred to the act of engaging employees in frontline idea generation as a "Shifting of Ownership" where a bottom-up leadership style "pulls up" instead of "pushing down" responsibility for making the business better. He provides a value-based guide to exceptional performance by fundamentally understanding the relationship between an employee's level of willingness to work for you and your customer's willingness to buy your products. His work to define the "value stick" is contemporary and scientific. When done right, providing both the responsibility AND recognition of obstacles in the way of achieving desired results can create more favorable working conditions. In the case study where he referenced some of my work, the institution of listening and acting on employee ideas was described as a deliberate and thoughtful discipline that paid off. Yes, the employee experience and customer experience are directly related.

Listening to those working on the frontline comes from a deep form of respect. I learned this as a field service engineer taking care of MRI equipment early in my career. Being avid troubleshooters, and often working alone in the middle of the night, we had to come up with solutions to problems every single day. I also worked on learning HOW to listen. I still work on my listening skills, even though my husband may disagree.

I was fortunate to have corporate-trained design thinking, workouts, brain-storming, crowd-sourcing, and formal leadership training which provided many opportunities to fine-tune my ears and mind. I also have an innate sense that folks on the frontline have the best intelligence as to what is going on.

I suppose I found too many board rooms where leaders espoused the truth, only to be enthralled by the brilliance of someone who stepped up to enlighten about with the reality of what was actually happening with customers. The further up in leadership I went, the further away I felt from the true reality. This really bothered me. To stay connected to customers and employees, I had to go below deck. This is a golden rule noted in John Kotter's *Leading Change*[28], which is one of my beloved guides. His eight steps to leading change (see more info on leading change in Chapter 9) are a proven method for countless firms, and are endorsed by Harvard. Personally, utilizing a 'Kotter-esque' approach to leading change has proven successful for me in manufacturing, financial transaction processing, and call center environments time after time.

To make transformational change, we need to produce broad-based action. We achieve this when the employees required to act are the ones who suggest it in the first place. Problem identification and solutions to customer and employee dissatisfaction are found on the frontline where the real work is taking place. This is not only about simple problems such as who changes the lightbulb, but also the bigger ones we need to solve in order to grow revenue, increase profit, gain market share, and so on. The answers usually exist within the minds of those closest to the work.

If You Don't Ask You Won't Get Anywhere

Case in point, some years ago, I was holding an employee roundtable with a group of agents in a call center at a large firm. We had discussed the business results, a new time off policy, and a couple of other sundry items. I always liked to save time at the end for questions and suggestions from the team. Sometimes there would be silence and people looking down at their shoes wondering when they could go on break. If I left enough of a pause in the air, and cajoled them a bit with open-ended questions, someone would inevitably speak up.

This time, one smart agent spoke up, "Why can't we just fax our customer the communications? They really don't want our phone calls. They get annoyed when I call out to them." The direct manager of this group was with us at the table and responded rather bureaucratically, stating it was a regulatory requirement to make the call. Note, I hate bureaucracy. Actually, to be really honest, I loathe it. It makes my skin crawl, my lip snarl, and my stomach twist. But, I've learned to have fun with it and you can too.

I responded to the statement: "Oh, really? Show me where I can read up on this regulation. I want to ensure I am fully versed and absolutely compliant."

What happened next was predictable. There was no regulation stating we specifically needed to make a phone call. There was only opinion, beliefs, and stances on the mode of communication required. Those agents and I now had something powerful. We had customer sentiment: real, direct, customer voices telling us they didn't want the call. We ran with this one. We did exhaustive research, stakeholder evaluations, compliance reviews, and business process changes. We followed through on this agent's idea. It saved the company millions of dollars and made customers and employees much happier.

A key point here is not only to listen and make change, but also to set the tone and create a culture for innovation. MIT recently published a story on this topic[29]. They identified four basic team culture types: distressed, comfortable, anxious, and innovative. Each of the types reflects a high and low emphasis on psychological safety AND intellectual honesty, which together determine the organization's relative ability to innovate. Many leaders understand the need for psychological safety, but may not be familiar with intellectual honesty. The authors refer to it as healthy debate AND team members proactively volunteering ideas. I call it respecting their intellect, and caring enough to ask and wait for an answer. By making it "okay" to speak up and setting an expectation of employees submitting ideas, Model Team Methodology™ effortlessly allows learning and innovation to occur.

The Employee Innovation System

So, how do you go about eliciting ideas from your team in an intellectually honest and respectful way? Do you go to the frontline once a month and get intel? Do you host a quarterly roundtable discussion? Do you hire a consultant to do a study? How about opening up a good old suggestion box? Well, I suppose all of those may work as long as you do those things AND you act on the information you receive.

What about the form and content of the ideas? How do you keep the roundtable from becoming a griping session? How do you prevent the suggestion box from filling up with requests to give everyone a raise? Let me tell you, there is a way to harness the intellect of your team and make real progress with it.

I have found the best way to engage employees and to create repeatable employee-led innovation is by following these three basic steps (see Figure 4):

Step 1. Request and Acknowledge Ideas

Step 2. Review and Prioritize Each One

Step 3. Act and Track without Fail

Figure 4-Employee Innovation Cycle

Step 1: Request and Acknowledge Ideas

Begin by defining macro business impact areas where you want to engage your team to improve AND create a fail-safe acknowledgment process. Structure a simple input form to collect the necessary data, including the area of impact, frequency of occurrence, proposed solution, and submitter's demographics. Each of these fields must be filled out by the submitter, especially their proposed solution to the issue.

When someone has to tell you not only what the problem is, but also what they would suggest doing to remedy it, the wheels start turning. You move from complaints into creativity. Perhaps you could structure your input form to capture ideas from employees for improving areas such as external (customer) and internal (employee) experiences. Maybe you add a macro commercial segment such as sales to increase revenue, or efficiency to provide a better operating margin. Depending on your industry, you may want to include a selection for safety, or product quality. It is up to you to decide the right input categories, but whatever you do, keep them, and the input form super simple. Two to four macro areas are plentiful. The last thing you want is to create a hurdle at the entry point. In one of my first jobs gathering employee ideas for improvement, I utilized a spreadsheet and manually entered them during meetings and interviews, and when they were sent to me by email. I shared the spreadsheet in an open forum and tracked progress regularly. In another team, we used Post-it notes and stuck them on the wall with our value stream map. I learned a lesson on this one; ensure you get the good kind of sticky notes, or add tape, otherwise, they fall off the wall. Actually, the tape is important, but seriously, the most important imperative is <u>do not lose someone's idea.</u> Being careless with employee idea submissions will derail your innovation train quicker than you can say choo-choo.

'Engaging the team in
innovation is fun'

The employee idea system works just as easily, if not better, online. I have witnessed a simple database tool that began as index cards submitted into an unused paint bucket. Both were effective, it's just that, when using the paint can method, it took more time to process the ideas. Most teams don't have too much trouble starting an exercise like this. Where they tend to fall is in the acknowledgment and tracking. Nothing kills an innovation program faster than employees feeling like they are talking to a brick wall. (I may say this at least one more time as it is really important, so bear with me.)

The acknowledgment need not be sophisticated. Assign a unique number to each idea submitted and send the employee a simple email saying, "Thanks for submitting your idea. We have received it and tagged it as number (X). You can request updates referencing this number (X) as it moves through the process." You can automate this process to make it easy on everyone; just don't miss the opportunity to make it personal. Anything you can do to ensure the employee's direct supervisor is engaged in the acknowledgment is going to benefit everyone involved. Remember, getting the ideas to start rolling in a structured way allows for easier sorting, and acknowledging them keeps your pipeline flowing.

Ensure you request ideas from every team member, regularly. You can use the regular close of daily huddles to ask for submissions. You can integrate it into staff meetings. Anytime you hear someone gripe about this, that, or the other thing, ask them if they have submitted their idea. This will train behavior.

You can run a contest to get the ball rolling. Although, be a bit careful on the game-playing. I'd caution you not to make rewards a habit for teammate's submissions. I remember having a graduate student ask me about providing rewards for ideas during one of our case study reviews at MIT. It was made clear by the Professor this is not a good idea. Providing ideas to improve the business is not a goal, it is an expectation. While you want to have lots of good ideas coming in, paying folks to participate is not the way to reward this behavior. There are plenty of other opportunities for reward when you get to the implementation stage (see Chapter 10 for more on this topic). Not only will rewarding inputs dilute the expectation of creating an innovative culture, but it could also become costly. In a recent HBR article[30], global marketing and advertising company Dentsu notes employees were more driven to bring forth new ideas by "company-wide visibility and a strong and selfish urge to get rid of boring tasks."

I have to agree as I have found the reward of realizing one's self-worth to be greater than any other monetary prize. Whatever you do, start by asking, then follow up 100% of the time. Let the submitter know you have received their idea along with transparency about where it is in the funnel. This is a crucial step. You must acknowledge each and every one to demonstrate respect for the effort and intellect put into it. There will undoubtedly be a lot of ideas coming in once you begin asking. It is critical to let people know they have been heard, and furthermore, to let them know what happens next.

Step 2: Review and Prioritize

A good cadence is to review and sort each of the employee's ideas at least weekly. The KPO can lead this exercise and train each of your Model Team Leaders how to do it as well. We want to prioritize the ideas during this process as well. I suggest using an impact versus effort grid (see Figure 5). It is a simple tool where you assess each of the ideas submitted against the four criteria of the grid (Effort vs. Impact). Ideas landing in the bottom right box, High Impact with Low Effort, are the 'Just Do It' ones, such as the time zone clock idea from Chapter 4. Ideas in the top right box will typically require further evaluation and resources to proceed, such as the faxing idea mentioned earlier. Ideas in the top and bottom left boxes could be easy wins, or they might be dismissed, given the low impact on your business. In my experience, it is not unusual to see upwards of 60% of ideas categorized for no action. This is actually a good thing as you must be able to say what you are **not** going to do as well as what you are going to do.

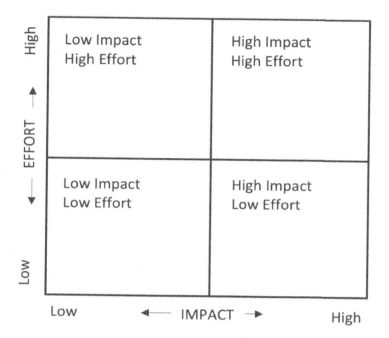

Figure 5 – Impact versus Effort Grid

Prioritizing what to work on is a key skill we need to have and impart to our teams. We also need to ensure we provide complete transparency about where the idea is in the process. It is okay to let a submitter know their idea is not proceeding, just let them know why, and, if we can, walk them through the assessment process so they can fully understand it.

Provide the team with a running count of ideas submitted, assessed, in progress, dismissed, and completed in an obvious and reliable manner. The team's huddle board is an ideal location. Refer to Chapter 5 for more info on utilizing visual dashboards to communicate frontline idea status to the entire group.

Step 3: Act and Track

Without fail, we must act and track all ideas. When I say we, I mean us, the leaders and our staff. In Chapter 3, I described setting up a KPO. They have an important role here. The skills needed to manage projects must exist in your KPO. To be clear, they are not going to own all the projects, but they are teachers and leaders. They will need to facilitate and teach your frontline managers and ambassadors how to assess the incoming ideas using the impact versus effort method. They will also need to be somewhat of a watchdog to ensure every single submission is acknowledged, and progress is made. I have seen the KPO take the lead in executing the hardest and largest initiatives. After all, our frontline managers and employees do have full-time jobs serving customers. However, giving a good dose of project work to the frontline is healthy. It allows them to pursue their vision for making the business better.

Keep track of every idea from the start (funnel) through to the finish (dismissal or execution) status. Make this data known throughout the team. I had success holding weekly reviews with the KPO, frontline Model Team managers, and supporting staff. It was a meeting we actually looked forward to. It was energizing to hold ourselves accountable and see the progress we were making.

Sometimes the news was not so great, for instance when project due dates slipped, or a big obstacle was discovered. The simple act of the team convening every single week and working together to make real change for the business was highly satisfying. The smiles on people's faces when big new revenue streams were discovered were joyful. We enjoyed laughter when hearing a goofy project name or learning about a failure that had turned into a "doh!" moment. Sometimes, I had to hold back tears of pure joy observing the growth of people who became stronger presenters and business leaders. They learned what worked and what didn't from each other. The business acumen of the entire group increased. We supported one another in this weekly working meeting., which was full of intellectual honesty and healthy debate.

Getting through all the ideas in a timely fashion can be difficult. One year, I saw over 1,500 ideas come through from 700 unique employees. That is a lot of acknowledging, sorting, prioritizing, and executing. It really does help to automate some or all of the administrative parts, so that, with a click of a button, one can see what is submitted, in process, and complete. It's not hard work, it just takes discipline.

We want to integrate the frontline idea processes at any time before embarking on starting our Model Teams as long as we have the resources to manage with 100% follow-up. Don't try to launch Model Teams without putting the employee innovation system in place. I found it easier to start the frontline innovation system at the same time as the first Model Team. This allowed us to get the cadence, sequencing, and execution right. It was also then easier to scale to the next team too.

If you want to learn more about employee-based idea systems, you could check in with The Gartner®[31] group. In April 2018, they set up a form of this employee innovation process to teach their members how to create better rep experiences. A colleague and I hosted a webinar for them as well, sharing our experience of how we were making work easier for the reps by engaging them in the innovation processes.

For those with frontline service teams, we know the customer service issues coming in are not getting easier. All the easy stuff is being handled by AI and automation via apps. Our teams are now more like technical troubleshooters in support of customers. They have a lot to share with you about what is happening. Go listen and engage and you will discover a gold-mine of engagement and positive change.

"Opportunity is missed by most people because it is dressed in overalls and looks like work. *-Thomas A. Edison*

Idea icon: Freepik via Flaticon.com

Model Leader Reflection–Engaging Employees in Innovation

1. What are you doing to request ideas (and solutions) from your team?
2. Are you acknowledging ideas and do employees confirm they are being heard?
3. Are the ideas reviewed and prioritized regularly?
4. Do you act on and track the idea pipeline?

Chapter 8

Creating Ambassadors... To Teach, Manage Projects, and Grow Talent

Franklin had a smile and gait that made everyone around him, including me, light up. Maybe it was the bow tie he sometimes wore to our meetings or the sight of his skinny physique stark against the 15-foot high whiteboard. Or, perhaps it was the way he pushed the bridge of his glasses up with his nervous energy and giggled. Something about this guy made those around him feel optimistic that there was a way forward, a promise of something better than our past.

Imagine someone like Franklin is one of the first ambassadors you recruited from the frontline to join your KPO. During a six–to–nine–month secondment, a handful of high-potential employees will be brought into a development program to learn continuous improvement, change management, and basic leadership. They will spend 50% of their time in the KPO learning, teaching, and managing projects. The balance of their time will be spent back doing their current job. We want to ensure their current skills do not get lost and need them to help with customers during peak times. Meanwhile, you will be preparing them for the future.

Ambassadors are put in place as the execution arm of the major innovation projects and trainers for the frontline. Their main role is making change, and making it stick. Before anyone can be chosen for an ambassador assignment, they need to demonstrate that they want and are ready for the role. Mirroring the selection process of Model Teams, the role of ambassador is obtained through a selection committee. Anybody can apply, as long as, 1) they are in good standing with their performance and behavior rating, and 2) they have the support of their supervisor. There is a simple form the applicants are required to submit along with a thoughtful improvement idea. Everyone who applies delivers a five-minute maximum presentation of their idea to improve the business and their readiness to execute it. The presentation must convey a grasp of the problem definition, likely causation, and benefits in terms of dollars and cents. After all, the language of business is finance, and thus, they need to show us they can understand it.

Their presentation does not have to be sophisticated, in fact, we want to coach them to keep the PowerPoint to a minimum and focus on outcomes. One difference to the Model Team selection process is that the candidate has to do the presentation on their own. Because they are vying to be the face of your KPO to their peers, it is important they demonstrate the ability to stand in front of an audience and deliver a message. Almost all of them will be noticeably nervous at the review. Most ambassador hopefuls have never presented in a business setting. With only five minutes to convey their message, and a panel of leadership staring back at them, one has to wonder why they would be interested in taking this risk.

They come forward because they are hopeful. These bright-eyed potential candidates are seeking opportunity. Opportunity to get away from the daily grind. Opportunity to learn something new. Opportunity to make a difference. Opportunity for promotion. Opportunity period.

The folks who come forward want a change for themselves and the business. It might not be readily apparent to most people just how much opportunity there can be for the ambassadors. After three years of running the program at my last firm, the promotion rate for these ambassadors was almost 100%! More than 9 of 10 frontline employees who put their necks out there to help the greater good, will see it turn into a positive thing for themselves in terms of higher pay and promotion. They become your succession funnel. The ambassadors will advance and people will notice. They do such good work.

Your KPO will be gaining traction and credibility with the frontline as a result.

'Provide employees
opportunity to grow'

What Do They Do Exactly?

Deciding what projects to work on can be overwhelming. The funnel of employee innovation is never-ending. Ideas for better customer experiences, product quality, and employee work processes will come to your group non-stop. The ideas that have the most potential return and that require the highest levels of effort are managed by the KPO. Most often, a bigger impact project born from the ambassador's home team is managed by them and their supervisor. However, as there is always a larger number of teams versus ambassadors, choosing the right ideas to work on becomes a process.

It can be frustrating to have so much to do and not enough resources to handle it. If you have just a couple of ambassadors working half of their time, and two other project leads in the KPO, you will have to bucketize and prioritize what gets worked on every week. Choosing what to work on is easier if you have clear goals to align to. I mentioned the importance of leaders creating and articulating goals in Chapter 5. Not only are they critically important for setting KPIs for our dashboards, but they are also a true north reference to guide our innovation efforts. With clear goals outlined, the job of sorting, ranking, and choosing the projects KPO ambassadors should work on is much easier.

Once the work is decided, it is assigned to an individual project manager for accountability. An operating mechanism with a disciplined cadence to review the status of projects is put in place. Every group I have worked with maintained a highly visual way one could go to see progress of the projects being worked on. In one team, there was a large, dedicated conference room with the entire service delivery value stream map pinned to the four walls. From request for quote, through remittance. The team had taken the time to outline the steps, how long each took, and the yield of its service delivery.

Generally, there are bright bursts plastered along the map highlighting areas of improvement opportunities. These are the places where the current value for the customer, employee, and business is sub-optimal. Above the map are details of the main projects being worked on, with owner, timeline, and status.

In one group, there were ambassadors who worked on the details of the projects, reporting to a Master Black Belt (MBB). There were around five MBBs who served as the collective KPO leadership for a cross-functional business improvement program. These folks possessed continuous improvement project management expertise and formal qualifications in Six Sigma and/or Lean. These qualifications provided them the opportunity to lead ambassadors and resolution of complex continuous improvement projects. The ambassadors looked up to the MBBs for examples of career progression opportunities.

> ***Master Black Belt (MBB)***:
> *a role characterized by significant continuous improvement and/or design expertise for the purpose of managing projects and programs to reduce waste and deliver the utmost value to customers. Certification can be achieved through a reputable training program.*

In another group, the place to see what was going on was on the production floor. Right next to a big whiteboard with the key performance indicators of the manufacturing group, there was another that clearly outlined the active projects, help needed, and recent wins. These two boards were strategically placed en route to the lunch room along a corridor that saw a lot of employee traffic. The daily shift stand-ups and KPO review sessions were held there. A key part of the success was the communication with everyone as to what projects were being worked on and the status of each of them—with full transparency.

The ambassadors receive much more visibility using these open forum project boards and review methods. While it can be intimidating at first, they quickly become more comfortable with being immersed in this operating style. I found it is great for tours too. Both internal and external clients can be shown the boards during visits. It provides transparency and authenticity to our work.

How Do I Afford Ambassadors?

You may be questioning how you can afford to create ambassadors from a team that is already stretched too thin. It is a real dilemma and a valid question. Many times, I had to prioritize the need to make cuts in one area in order to invest in others. What works is to clearly state your intentions, realize that something the team did well in the past may be impacted, and set expectations for better results in the future. Give yourself and the team some slack to invest in finding improved efficiencies for the longer term. Above all, provide air cover to those willing to take the leap with you.

Believe it or not, the biggest hurdle I have found is actually the direct supervisory and management team letting go of their "A" players for the greater good. There was a moment in my past when a supervisor had been prioritizing achieving her metrics over developing her team and refused to support a team member in applying for an ambassador role. Was the supervisor wrong for making decisions to benefit her customers? She had her priorities clearly articulated by those above her and understood them. The issue this supervisor and many others face is that they are missing the opportunity to create an "AND" equation.

As leaders, we have to figure out how to make the metrics AND develop our people. In fact, the more we do the latter, the better it gets. Case in point... the supervisor I mentioned here did eventually support her employee as an ambassador. Her leader was coached to provide her with the air cover needed which helped a lot. The employee spent 50% of their time on their secondment. They were learning, doing, and teaching others as an ambassador in the KPO. The other 50% of their time was at their service desk job.

The lunchroom conversation with this new ambassador started buzzing. Suddenly, there was more energy in the group, due to this assignment. Other teammates wanted to know the inside scoop and were actively watching to see what might happen. This was something different and new. One of their own was making a move and it was exciting. As the ambassador began to learn and teach, the supervisor became something of a legend too. Association matters. She was vested in their success because it also belonged to her. And the best part was that positive changes came more quickly to this ambassador's team, as they were the first to know, and usually one of the test beds for new ideas.

The team also became more engaged as a unit. HBR shared a study in 2016 noting, "The more people you energize, the higher your work performance. This occurs because people want to be around you. You attract talent, and people are more likely to devote their discretionary time to your projects. They'll offer new ideas, information, and opportunities to you first."[32] Yes, it's true, I saw some leaders trying to hold their teammates back from applying, but in the end, they never won. In fact, they usually lost more than just one teammate.

Creating Virtual Ambassadors

To create and sustain ambassadors in the work-from-home or virtual model you need trust, and a great learning environment. Here's a newsflash... it is harder to curate ambassadors in a remote setting. Seeing someone eye to eye, not via Zoom, but actually in person, facilitates better communication. There, I said it. Working virtually is actually harder to do. It doesn't deter from the reality that work-from-home is not going away and that I endorse it 100%. It is just harder. Here are some things we can do to make it work.

Facing uncertainty without the benefits of being able to communicate fully is brutal. I learned a long time ago that communication is only 7% verbal.[33] That's right. Only 7% of what you think you are saying is done through your words. The vast majority of what we communicate is done through our eyes, hand gestures, posture, and tone. There is a big emptiness of critical non-verbal communication in email by the way. Think about that next time you choose to send an email rather than picking up the phone. But, I digress and you need to know how to create working remote ambassadors. Let me propose a couple of scenarios for you to digest.

Situation 1:

Kelly is an up-and-coming superstar representative, who is pursuing a bachelor's degree in nursing. You know Kelly will eventually leave the company to follow her calling. Her talent is endless and you want to help her grow as much as possible. She had become an ambassador within the first two years of employment. Kelly learned how to be an ambassador on site. She trained others both virtually and in person. Her Sensei in your KPO managed both on-site and virtual Model Teams, and thus she did as well. Kelly is working on a particularly large improvement project to determine the root cause and resolve a major customer pain point. Perhaps your customers are calling multiple times due to a low first-call resolution rate.

The data collection for this issue is not too difficult given the advanced technology of your operations. Analyzing and digging deeper into the case details requires the bulk of the effort. As Kelly is going to school, and working nearly full-time, flexibility in her schedule is very important. During the analysis phase of the project, she worked from home. It allowed her to focus and save the commute. When your weekly review comes around, she is present in the conference room. She knows how to balance remote and in-person work. Kelly is highly effective in her role as she understands the right communication lanes to follow to complete the job. By the way, your company might provide her and all employees with a healthy tuition benefit. This is often a good employment strategy 101.

Situation 2:

This one involves an up-and-coming rock star call center rep, Calvin, but is more of a cautionary tale. He is renowned for the volume of calls he can handle along with his positive rapport with customers. He has been with your team about two years when he takes on the role of ambassador. He starts out in the office and yet makes it very clear he wants to work remotely in the long run, in order to drop and pick up his children from school. Calvin learned on-site and provided training to others both in person and remotely. His program

94

management skills are not as strong nor instinctive; however, the team feels he can learn them fairly quickly.

He is assigned a large improvement project to assist fellow reps in handling calls more effectively. Given his background, it is a great fit and there is a major need to deliver productivity for the business and efficiency for your clients. The base data for the project is readily available, but, as with Kelly's work, the analysis requires digging deeper and observation of actual customer interactions in progress. All the technology is there to listen in on calls from afar, so he asks to work remotely in order to have a more focused space in which to do the work.

You grant the request. When the weekly reviews come around, Calvin dials into them. He makes excuses about not having much progress to share. You listen for the first two weeks, then it gets old. There is no real work being done remotely by him. He is not able to deliver, for a couple of reasons. First, he did not possess the basic time and project management skills required before he was allowed to go solo. Second, he did not have the right motivation to work remotely. To Calvin, it was a free pass to get paid for not working, as he believed no one would pay attention when he was not in the office. The assignment does not end well for him. You might have to terminate him for falsifying records, including his own time sheet.

The Point Is To Provide Them Skills

The main difference in these two scenarios may seem elementary. Kelly possessed the basic skills needed to do the job, no matter where it was being performed. Calvin on the other hand, did not. He lacked basic organizational skills. However, you wonder if you could have helped Calvin develop these skills; might he then have been able to do the job? You think the reason he may have cheated would be due to his own fear of inadequacy? Marie Mitchell, an associate professor of management who was involved in research at the University of Georgia found, "It's the desire for self-protection that primarily causes employees to cheat…Employees want to look valuable and productive, especially if they think their job is at risk."[34]

'Develop employees for future success'

Isn't this interesting? It reinforces what you have known for some time. People don't come to work to do a bad job. It is the environment. It is their skills coupled with the expectations placed on them, as well as their boss, that determine their happiness and success at work. You probably can't train everybody in everything they need to do a job. That's what college and other supplementary courses are for. However, it is a leader's job to ensure they have the right skills or can gain them quickly, in order to perform. In scenario two above, you need to consider it a management failure to have let Calvin proceed to become an ambassador. Maybe you rationalized your ability to train him in project management without a clear understanding of his basic readiness for the role. Could he have been more successful if you had given him time to learn some of the basic organizational skills, through a college course, and practical team projects before putting him in the role? It would have been a minimal investment for a lifetime of return.

Ambassador icon image: Noomtah via Flaticon.com

Model Leader Reflection–Building Bench Strength

1. Is your KPO ready to mentor and train an ambassador?
2. Have you discussed the benefit of the ambassador program with your staff and superiors?
3. Is your project prioritization process sufficient to prevent overload of the KPO and ambassadors?
4. Do you have interest from the frontline in ambassadorship?

Chapter 9

Coaching Change Up, Down, and Sideways... the Art of Change Acceleration

You are going to need change management skills in order to transform your team. Whether you decide to follow the Model Team approach or not, leading change is a leader's job. One of my favorite discussions about change happened during an interview. I had decided it was time to move on from my green-field manufacturing start-up adventure and head to a place where I could follow my service roots. I had enjoyed and grown significantly in over three years of leading the new circuit board manufacturing facility development. I knew it was time for a change when day after day I awoke to face the same challenges as the day before. I needed something different.

My heart and passion have always been in service businesses, and there was a role I wanted. I was being interviewed by a Senior Vice President (SVP) and was in one of the final rounds to get the job. This SVP was a tough cookie. Smart, sharp, respected, with significant experience across the company, she had become an officer of this Fortune five company in her forties. This was a pretty big deal for me and I was nervous. It was a phone interview and we knew each other fairly well, having worked together in the past. Her last question during this session was the one I cannot forget. She said, "Tell me about change and how you approach it."

No kidding, this is one of my most beloved topics of discussion, and so on I went on to answer her question. I articulated, change is one of those things you must not avoid. I do not recall the exact words I responded with, but it was probably something along the lines of *"Change or die"*[35]. It is not about changing without thought or incessant activity, but with purpose, strategy, and deliberate execution.

I also shared a key point I know to be true...you must be able to recognize when NOT to change. Don't change when a) you are on the path, and perhaps get knocked down, or encounter a large obstacle; b) when you are changing for change's sake and not the good of the business; or c) the purpose is not helping customers or people. Don't change when change is not congruent with your morals, values, or integrity. It may take some grit, but it is wise in these situations to "Stay the Course", and not waver in your intentions.

I got the job and it led to my first foray as General Manager. There was much change headed my way. For the next two years, I led a huge transformation of the service contracting and invoice team. I also went through a major transformation at home, with the birth of our son. My husband and I were in our early forties and had nearly given up on the prospect of having children. Luck, and perhaps divine intervention, provided us with the best gift of our lives. Talk about change; what a wake-up call (pun intended) it is to have a newborn late in life. When we were discharged from the hospital the nurses told me our new baby boy was going to need to eat every two hours. The corporate gal in me assumed they meant between the hours of 8 a.m. and 5 p.m. However, I adapted quickly to the 24x7 role of caring for a newborn. Becoming a parent provides a great lesson in dealing with change.

The Change Process

I believe in taking a structured and pragmatic approach to change and mostly follow the path of John Kotter's "Leading Change"[36] framework. His eight-stage process of executing major change is clearly outlined and can be followed by anyone. Here are the steps:

1. Establish a sense of urgency

2. Create a guiding coalition
3. Develop a vision and strategy
4. Communicate the change vision
5. Empower broad-based action
6. Generate short-term wins
7. Consolidate gains and produce more change
8. Anchor new approaches in the culture

From the point of knowing you need to change, you must light a fire within yourself and the people you need with you on the journey. You need to visualize what you will achieve and outline a strategy to get there. You need to communicate from Monday through Sunday and via numerous channels to reach your constituents. You need to craft early wins, execute, adapt, and celebrate. And most of all, you need to sustain the change once you have made it.

Case In Point

According to a case study conducted by the Stanford Graduate Business School, Agilent was formed as a stand-alone $8 billion dollar start-up from several successful units of the Hewlett-Packard (HP) firm in 1999.[37] The Agilent CEO wanted to take the best of HP's culture and practices, known as "the HP Way," and grow exponentially with external focus. Just six months into it, they were already ranking in the top 50 of Forbes best companies to work for, nearly 20 points higher than their HP brethren. They had the largest initial public offering Silicon Valley had ever seen at $2.1B. Their employee base had mostly migrated from HP and was 46,000 strong. They were focused and ready.

At the start, their change management plan was robust, and working. They had the right vision, people, and execution. They had chosen to move away from the HP legacy of a decentralized organizational structure in pursuit of a more contemporary shared services model. They were swiftly undertaking a massive change management and integration exercise.

By mid-2001, some of their key markets had shifted significantly. Revenue started declining rapidly. Despite their intent to be even more externally and competitively focused, they were now caught up internally in cost-cutting measures. They lost their external focus, or at least their ability to forecast and react to changing economic conditions. They were facing inevitable layoffs.

Unfortunately, in a time of great uncertainty, their communications weakened rather than being ramped up. Leadership clamped down rather than delegating. One of the best elements inherited from HP, the entrepreneurial spirit, withered away in the employees who now were Agilent. There was simply too much chaos among this new firm.

What we can learn from this case is that a change plan is only a plan. External forces need to be monitored and plans adapted. Communication is king, especially in times of crisis. And perhaps most important, change management needs to play a central function, working as an integrator, facilitator, and scout. It is my belief that, had Agilent maintained the autonomy of decentralized business units with a centralized integration team leading the change plan, they may have yielded better results. Perhaps a Model Team method may have worked for them if they had focused on one part of the business at a time to form a shared services relationship. I do know one of the secret ingredients in the recipe for successful Model Teams is the entrepreneurial spirit of frontline teams with the autonomy to run their business and a supportive central KPO. It is this push and pull balance that makes change work in an ever-changing world.

Deciding AND Doing

I changed roles when I came back from maternity leave to lead the integration of a healthcare equipment firm's $2-billion service businesses. There were eight distinct business groups and the company wanted them to become one cohesive unit. I am pretty sure we heard cliches like, "We're going to leverage our synergies," and, "We need to be one face to the customer." While these statements were made, they were never going to be the call to action nor the guiding coalition needed to get over 2,000 employees on board with a massive change initiative like this.

This was a textbook case for leading change. The company was full of trained Six Sigma and change acceleration process champions. I was one of them, utilizing the toolsets on a routine basis. One really smart guy on our team suggested we utilize Hoshin Kanri methods (refer to Chapter 5 on technique how-to's) to organize our strategic goals and deployment. This worked quite well in herding the senior leadership team into articulating the main value we wanted to deliver by integrating these eight business units. When another super smart guy on our team encouraged me to read the book *Five Frogs On A Log*[38], my mission and approach to this change became crystal clear. There are a few standout points from this book that triggered a shift in my thinking including:

- "Knowing best practices are based on past conditions."
- "There is no such thing as a merger of equals."
- "Culture can't be blended like a milkshake."
- "The new conditions wrought by a merger often cry out for a fresh point of view."
- "Successful communication of change begins by understanding that the questions following any announcement revolve around one central theme: "'How does this affect me?'"

I know first-hand that sales and service people can take their frustrations to customers, especially when they are unclear about the last bullet point above. There is a direct correlation between employee morale and customer satisfaction.

The last thing I wanted to do was ignore the folks in the field. These were my people. My family. The field is where I came from and where I grew up. I knew they knew what was happening with customers. I also knew they didn't know what the integration would mean for them. I had to bridge this gap and reduce anxiety and uncertainty for all. This was a point in my career where my communication skills grew in leaps and bounds. Figuring out which communications were needed, with who, what, when, where and why, was a daily job.

I developed a strong rapport with the communications lead for the business and helped to leverage his polish and delivery. Content was really important. Everyone wanted to see the new organization charts. They wanted to know where cost-cutting would take place. They wanted to know about technology systems merging. We focused on the behavioral changes needed and stayed on point with our value drivers and progress therein. We listened and responded non-stop. I utilized that book as a guide with strategic goal deployment tools to rally the team, focus our execution, and deliver a highly successful integration in six months.

Incremental Change

Not every change we initiate is going to be transformational, although I hope all leaders will aim for at least one after they finish reading this book. We must make incremental changes regularly too. For example, let's say you need to make an improvement to your weekend staffing model. Not only is it hard to get folks to work the weekends, but these shifts also suffer high absenteeism and overtime rates. They are typically assigned to the newer associates because the tenured ones want to have better schedules. There may have been requests directly from the frontline to provide alternative work schedules such as four ten-hour or three twelve-hour shifts. Your workforce management team is guided by customer demand which is measured by the minute. This allows for good data coupled with human resources analysis. A side benefit discovered during the analysis is the fact that some of the teams are rotating to work weekends at least once per month, while others are not rotating at all.

In the spirit of equality, taking care of customers, and respecting employee tenure, a solution is devised by utilizing the data and a cross-functional team. The solution could require every associate to become part of the weekend schedule rotation. However, dedicated three twelve-hour and four ten-hour shifts from late Friday through early Monday morning time would be offered first. Much to your team's surprise, there are lots of takers for the Friday through Sunday shifts as employees can enjoy a condensed schedule and more days off. Once the dedicated weekend shift selection process is complete, the team moves on to fill the remaining 20% of weekend associate schedules. Surprisingly, you find the remaining employees only needed to work a weekend shift once every two months. For some, who had not worked weekends in a long time, the thought, or even a whisper of a change coming is not pleasant. There may be a heavy sense of entitlement in this group. However, for the other folks, there is relief, and hope. Although this change is minor in the larger scheme of your business, you manage it with urgency, a guiding coalition, clear purpose, comprehensive communication, and anchors to your team culture. You concentrate communications on the "How does this affect me?" question we knew all employees would ask. The change is a win-win. Weekend scheduling further stabilizes your 24x7 operations for customers and gives new flexibility to employees.

Change Curves and the Big Dip

When thinking about change management across a varied population, whether it is major or minor, I frequently refer to Diffusion of Innovations Theory[39]. The adoption curve as shown in Figure 6 explains this in a way I find easiest to convey.

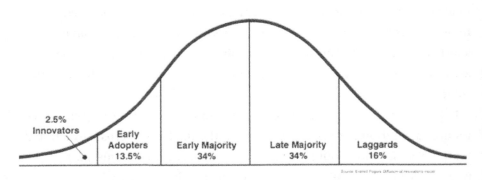

Figure 6–Diffusion of Innovation Adoption Curve

In any group, there are generally 16% or so who will innovate and adapt early on. These are the type of folks who always want to be on the cutting edge. They pre-order the next great gizmo and participate in beta software programs to tinker with them, just because it is cool and they want to be first. These are the folks on the far left-hand side of the curve. The vast majority of people, 68%, will be divided into early and late majority. These are the two big chunks in the middle of the curve. They are the general population who kind of flock like sheep, some going more quickly than others, but going with the flow. Then there's the 16% who lag behind. They are on the far right-hand side of the curve. This group must see the evidence, be certain it is safe, and have strong opinions on why they should or shouldn't do something. In the case of the change to weekend shift work, it was vital to understand the different groups. We have to ensure their views are understood and addressed with proper communication in the change plan. It is OK to focus on the 84%, but do not ignore the 16% of laggards. They can provide some of the richest intel on why your change might be flawed. Respect this perspective and listen, so you can gain valuable insights for your risk mitigation plan. By contrast, they can become your biggest headache if you let them. Stay focused and help the team adapt.

Undeniably, when making any significant change, one of the biggest things people get wrong is not planning for a potential drop in performance during the process. There are some who say an inevitable dip is a myth.[40] They believe it is more of a "mind over matter" issue, because, if you plan better, state your intentions, and execute flawlessly, you will avoid the dip. They point out many firsts have been achieved when people let go of perceived barriers. You can run a four-minute mile they say. I would like to believe I follow this vision in optimistic perpetuity. Practically speaking though, and based on multitudes of published research,[41] a dip will happen as the organization unlearns and relearns new modes. Agilent was a huge example of this going wrong. I say, plan for it. Your job is to minimize the depth and duration of the change curve and to sustain the gains as shown in Figure 7. You can do this with good planning, communication, and training before, during and after the change is made.

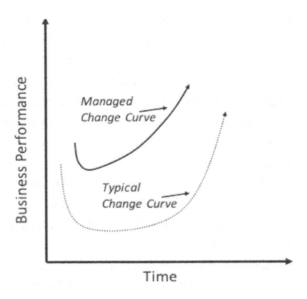

Figure 7–Change curves

No matter how transformational the change is, a simple outline of what we are planning to do provides grounding. Utilize the reflection questions below to ask yourself, and please, write down answers to these questions, in preparation for a major change. Communication during any change is crucial, but before we can do it, we need to articulate in our mind, and on paper, what exactly we are going to do and what we are going to say. Once this is clear, go forth and prosper.

System Change icon: Parzival 1997 via Flaticon.com

Model Leader Reflection–Communication Plan for Change

1. What is changing?
2. What exactly will be different from before (specific with metrics, organizational structure, etc.)?
3. Why is the change necessary?
4. How will it be deployed?
5. Who is affected, directly and indirectly?
6. Who is not affected, but needs to know?
7. When will it go into effect?
8. What are the communication rhythms and media types you will use?
9. Where can folks go to ask questions or get more information?

'Articulate a change to yourself
before communicating it with others'

Chapter 10

Leading Virtually... Trust is a Virtue and Communication is King

Recent events have forced many companies to enable a work-from-home model, whether they wanted to or not. I feel fortunate to have had extensive experience leading remote working teams. One benefit is that it enhanced my ability to lead through a crisis. Since the late nineties, having worked in truly global businesses, it was commonplace to have teleconferences with our overseas partners at all hours of the day and night. I worked on planes, trains, and in my dining room without ever really giving it a second thought. If there was a job to be done, I was going to make it happen. Post-pandemic, I reflected not just on how lucky I was to have had these global experiences, but particularly on two innate traits I had learned. In my experience, trust and communication are what makes or breaks a team, and this is even more true of a virtual one.

The 3 Cs

Let us start with communication. The act of writing down and communicating the nature of business goals, outcomes, and expectations is imperative in any work environment. I already talked about how important it is to articulate a change and wrap it up into a formal change plan. When working remotely, you have to communicate until you feel like a broken record.

One painful lesson I learned came during my experience working with a team in Japan. It was quite early in my professional career. Even though I read, researched, and even learned a bit of the Japanese language, I admittedly did not have the best grasp on cultural norms. I embarrassed myself during my first visit, by introducing myself as "MaryAnn-san." In Japanese culture, adding "san" to a person's name is a form of respect one can only receive, not take. I was basically introducing myself by saying, "Hello, I am the most revered!" My introduction was followed by modest laughter and a nudge from my colleague whispering, "You don't 'san' yourself." I never forgot this moment as it was not the best way to start out a professional meeting. I was much more astute following this episode, even if I was still naive.

After a large video conference session with the group, I proceeded to take action on what I assumed we had discussed and agreed to. This was because everyone around the table, including those in Japan, had nodded vehemently to the decision. Later on, I came to realize that the team in Japan nodded at everything. This gesture was more a sign of respect to, or at least acknowledgment of the person speaking, not necessarily an agreement to what they were saying. I learned the hard way to publish notes in writing as clearly and promptly as possible.

This led to the creation of program trackers, and metric dashboards, which most folks probably use today; but do they know why and what they are for? Simply put, they are to communicate and get everyone on the same page. I know this sounds obvious, but the reality is, especially in virtual working teams, communication is the key to success. When in doubt, remember the three Cs. Communicate. Communicate. Communicate.

If you have a team with a significant portion of employees who work remotely, you need to ensure your daily stand-ups, performance metrics, and project updates are performed digitally. Some of the basic Microsoft and Google tools will work just fine although connectivity challenges may be hard to avoid. Take the time to provide simple set-up instructions for your employees to get online and stay connected. You may find that one of your biggest challenges is team members not being well-versed in using these tools. Perhaps some of them are fine reading them digitally, but not in writing, via a spreadsheet for example. You may encounter resistance from remote employees in the use of video camera for online meetings. Don't let it be optional. Working remotely requires one to be present and presentable. You can and should specify for employees what being presentable means. Recognize the skills of your team and shore up any gaps to make communicating in the virtual world easier.

Before the digital tools, and the pervasiveness of virtual teams, I liked using a whiteboard and erasable marker. I actually still do. It is so simple. You pick up a pen and you write in a place everyone can see. This is what you must strive for in creating your Model Team. Imagine all you have is a simple whiteboard and marker. Whittle down what you want to achieve into only the must-know metrics and key points. Then, communicate them. Less is definitely more. **If you don't have one or two key goals you can recite off the top of your head at any moment, you need to hunker down and reflect on what it is you want to achieve.** See chapter 6 for more guidance on finding your key performance indicators. As your first virtual Model Team begins, it will be much easier for everyone to get in a rhythm if you are focused on a few key measures and have a time and place whereby everyone can get updates.

'Simple communication
is not simple'

The Big "T"

Now let's talk about the big "T"... Trust. Nothing is more important for teamwork. It is the number one dysfunction of a team,[42] followed by fear of conflict, lack of commitment, avoidance of accountability, and inattention to results – as eloquently outlined in the book *Five Dysfunctions of A Team*. I love this book. It has helped me align multiple teams to a true north. I find the trust factor to be the number one cause of disunity.

Remote work has only further tested a team's ability to trust one another. Just think about the aspects of someone's physical presence versus what they are delivering. When you see someone walking down the hallway in your office, you can easily form an impression of them being present, and therefore, you believe they must be working on something. After all, they did *come* to work. Unfortunately, I've seen plenty of folks messing around at work, even though they were in the office. Many, many years ago, one guy was literally snoring, so loudly you could hear him two cubicles over. It was not the first time. His presence in the office was not productive; in fact, it was the opposite for the entire team who were working around him.

The point here is akin to the five frogs riddle (for those who don't know this, refer to the beginning of Chapter 13). Just because one *decides* to come to work, doesn't mean they are *doing* the work. According to the most recent Work Trend Index published by Microsoft's Work Lab[43], 87% of global employees report that they are productive at work. However, 85% of global business decision-makers say that the shift to hybrid work has made it challenging to have confidence that people are being productive. How can this be? As the report's apt title asks, "*Isn't Remote Work Still Just Work?*" They provide some sound advice to engage your employees and end what they refer to as productivity paranoia. Model Team Methodology™ is a fantastic method with which to engage your team and deliver awesome productivity whether on-site or virtual.

I believe leader paranoia is synonymous with not trusting our people. We know trust is not a given. Through my experience I have learned to trust AND verify. We can only verify work is being done if we set out and monitor the work that needs to be done in the first place. This means articulating goals and utilizing key performance metrics to track progress. This is why I discussed communication before trust. If we are not a good communicator, our team is going to get mixed messages, and their ability to trust us is going to waver. In turn, if we do not listen to our team, by engaging them in innovation and the overall running of the business, we are not trusting them to achieve our goals.

Whether we work on site or virtually, trust and communication are the basis of leadership. These components are amplified when working virtually. There's a terrific book called, *The Year Without Pants*[44], in which the author describes their experience working completely virtually at WordPress. One of my favorite lines from this book is, "no method can magically make employees trust each other or their boss if they have good reason not to." He goes on to say, "...how you create, build, and sustain trust requires an exercise in evaluating your company culture." Committing to any team who demonstrate that they want to make things better for customers and employees is an act of trust. Create this and you will have more fun and get more done at work.

Which Mode is Better?

How do we decide whether working in person or virtually is best for our business? This is a widely debated topic with pros and cons for both. So many leaders had to move to a 100% virtual workforce during the 2020 pandemic. Those who had significant prior experience working remotely made the transition not only possible, but smoother. How many people can work remotely, and why it is even allowed was frequently debated prior to the crisis. On the one hand, you might have a high percentage of your team working at home and quite effectively. Higher employee and customer satisfaction measures might be noted in this group. On the other hand, internal stakeholders can doubt your virtual team's ability to be collaborative and productive.

We continue to wonder if working from home is productive and really necessary in order to retain the best talent. There are employees who are unable to relocate to a company-owned facility, and it adds cost to the business to move them. If you decide to retain them in a work-from-home model, you want to ensure they are 1) highly skilled, 2) tenured, and 3) self-directed. In the beginning, retaining them in a work-from-home scenario might have been a business survival decision as they had legacy knowledge you could not duplicate elsewhere. As time goes on, you witness how productive and flexible they are. Then, you realize working from home is also a way to attract a broader talent pool. You might also find it works to curb employee attrition.

You may be asking, "Can a KPO be led effectively in a remote setting." The answer is yes, and it can accelerate your employee engagement levels of remote teams as well. Leading requires empathy and understanding of the job being performed in the employee's physical setting. This doesn't mean you nor your KPO leader randomly go to an employee's house and inspect their office. It does mean you ask questions and provide resources to meet your employees where they are at. You can and should have virtual "Shark-tank" sessions and not just for the work from employees. Do it for groups in alternate cities, states, and even countries. You can also host in-person sessions for the teams to work together on larger projects. When employees see that you care, they are more engaged. Refer to Chapter 8 on managing virtual ambassadors.

Remote work is not without challenges. Personally, I like a hybrid approach with a portion of folks working from home, or a portion of the week worked from the physical office. Hybrid work offers the flexibility to adjust to labor and business conditions. In my experience, teamwork and camaraderie are not as strong when everyone is remote. It can be harder to run effective daily huddles. It is harder to get the whole team to engage in continuous improvement. It is definitely harder to train, especially for new employees. Hiring directly into a virtual role can feel nearly impossible if the candidate does not have significant experience. If your training methods have been adapted to a mostly virtual environment sooner, it might be easier. Given all of this, I would still offer a majority of the team virtual work, as it respects their choice and ability to be effective, no matter where they are located. And frankly, if we don't trust our employees to do the work we hired them for, why are they still working for us?

Honesty icon image: Freepik via Flaticon.com

Model Leader Reflection–Leading From Anywhere

1. What are your team's communication rhythms?
2. What could you do to enhance your digital communications and/or the team's competency in reading and writing them?
3. How would you rate the trust of your team with you and each other?
4. Which model is best for your business and employee needs: virtual, in person, or hybrid?
5. What could you do to improve your virtual leadership?

Chapter 11

Recognize, Reward, and Promote

One of my favorite comedy movies is *Meet the Fockers*[45] featuring Ben Stiller as Gaylord Focker. It is about a hilarious trip with his fiancée Pam and future in-laws to meet his parents. I love the "Wall of Gaylord" scene in which Robert De Niro, who plays Pam's dad, comments, "Oh, I didn't know they made ninth place ribbons..." Dustin Hoffman, playing a super proud Mr. Focker, has created a tribute wall for his son showcasing his accomplishments, responds, "Oh Jack, they got them all the way up to 10th place."

If you want to give out trinkets for all the good deeds folks on your team do, there are plenty of mugs and pencils with "I'm kind of a big deal" engravings to be found. I am not opposed to cool swag gear here and there, but we cannot confuse it with meaningful recognition, rewards, and career advancement. The US military is great at giving out awards. My husband was in the Army, my father in the Navy, and many military veteran colleagues along the way demonstrated to me the power of proper recognition. There is a rank and order to the pins and awards. There is a culture of pride and achievement. The entire process is ceremonial and meaningful. However, as Ash Carter, 25th Secretary of Defense, wrote, "America's military is the finest fighting force the world has ever known because of the people we attract to an all-volunteer force. But the traditions and rules that have strengthened the U.S. military over the last 250 years can, at times, make recruitment and retention difficult."[46]

They have learned to adapt to the needs of the newest generations, including broadening opportunities for women, enabling assignments to and from civilian corporations, and more lateral position movement. Even though we can clearly see the rank of a military person by the insignia on their uniform, not everyone wants to achieve five stars on their collar.

The recognition and rewards we provide to our team as leaders must be personal and congruent with goals, and they must provide opportunities for growth. Whatever we do here will be reflected directly in our retention strategies.

Focus on Behaviors and Deliverables

When thinking about recognition and rewards, I focus on the behaviors and deliverables we want to see. I find a lot of leaders struggle with encouraging recognition generally because they just don't do enough of it, or they are inconsistent. It can be even tougher to tackle the constructive side of any unwanted behaviors they witness.

I was recently coaching a woman on how to construct a performance improvement plan for a guy on her team who was continually failing at his work. She had hired him just over a year earlier, and directed his work, so it was even harder to accept he was not cutting it. His failure felt like her failure. She was struggling as he had many personal issues going on and found it difficult to get to the work issues. These types of conversations are tough. You need to have a heart and also run the business.

She and I reflected on the expectations of his role. I asked her to think about what she would put in a job ad for a replacement candidate and compare that to what he was currently delivering. Then I asked her to think about what she would say to herself if she was the one leaving because she failed to manage his performance. My point was to keep the goals, and personal accountability front and center. He might have needed a leave of absence to get his personal matters under control. Or he might have needed a different approach to accountability. Allowing anyone on our team to not deliver, be evasive, or be a jerk with others is disincentive behavior, not just with them, but for all those working alongside them.

I could relate to this woman first-hand as I have hired a few folks who failed in the job I hoped they could do. I have experienced failure in jobs I tried to do. Ultimately, the thing I said to my mentee that made the most impact was based on how she was rewarding this guy. "Are you rewarding him for not completing assignments on time with the ability to actually have less work because you and others are picking up the slack? Is he getting a year-end bonus simply because he is on the team even though he didn't pull his weight? As long as you are confident the goals are clear and you have provided him with ample learning to shore up any skill gaps he may have, what exactly are the consequences for him of not doing the job you hired him to do?" She paused and realized the only ones experiencing consequences were her and her boss. This conversation led her to have a more direct conversation and get the guy back on track. She created a time-based action plan with clear deliverables and expectations taking the best interests of the team and the key results her team needed to deliver to the business into consideration.

I remember leading a team years ago and thinking about the consequences of folks not doing the job they had been hired for. In fact, there were a gross number of absences, and people calling in sick. The rest of the team who were showing up for work were paying the price. We made a change to the attendance policy and announced it to the team. One guy in the back of the room stood up and clapped upon hearing the news. He was fed up with putting up with doing more work because of folks who didn't show up, yet still got paid. I am emphasizing the need for fairness in providing performance and behavioral feedback here, because if you don't shore up this side of your leadership equation, your recognition and rewards for a job well done are going to be unbalanced and mistrusted by your employees.

Create a Transparent Recognition Plan

We want to be clear about recognition and reward programs with our teams. Many corporations have big overarching recognition programs, and these are terrific. You might think about complementary plans to these with a more personalized local team recognition. What works is to draft a plan at the start of every year to ensure rewards drive the desired goals, and to ensure their sufficient recognition. Publish a simple program to the entire group outlining what, when, how, and why they can be recognized. My all-time favorite was called the "Everyday Hero" award. It was derived by nominations of the employees peer group. This gave it special meaning for the recipient as their peers understood first hand what it takes to get the job done. I don't recall if there was any financial reward. It didn't matter and was not necessary. The leader of the group recognized the importance of camaraderie, respect, and frontline leadership. Recognition of a job well done in a public way was, and still is, enough.

> "I have yet to find the man, however exalted his station, who did not do better work and put forth greater effort under a spirit of approval, than under a spirit of criticism."[47] —Charles Schwab

Consider intervals of monthly, quarterly, and annual awards as a starting point for your rewards and recognition program. Involve your leadership team in the setting of the criteria, and, of course, engage the frontline in the nomination processes whenever possible. You can add financial components to the awards if feasible but take a look at the book *1501 Ways to Reward Employees* for a multitude of other ideas. Of specific note, check out the highlighted story of Johnson & Johnson, about their work to ensure formal recognition programs were meaningful to employees. They surveyed their teams and made updates to their programs in response to what they heard. This is yet another way to engage your team in making work meaningful.

Advancement Opportunities

For many, the ultimate reward for doing a good job is an opportunity for advancement. Specialized training programs are wonderful for this purpose. They are especially helpful when they provide learning skills for the employee's next role. Nominating an employee to attend an exclusive leadership training session, or to learn the latest data analytics tools can be an incredible motivator. You might consider sponsoring someone to achieve Project Management Professional (PMP)®[48] – to reward great performance and to demonstrate belief in them for higher responsibilities ahead. This could help feed your KPO pursuits too!

As you implement Model Team Methodology™ in your groups it will be good to know you do not need a bucket of reward money to make folks feel appreciated. The attention, training, improvement of experiences, and most of all, respect for their intellect will be enough to engage your employees. There is also something about advancing to the next level that folks want too. Not everyone wants to move into a leadership position. Defining technical career paths and providing opportunity within them can be quite beneficial. Providing learning opportunities for people who want to grow their skills can benefit both them and the company.

Certification of Model Teams

Not surprisingly, about a year into your journey, each group may want to be more than just a Model Team. They want to experience a greater level of achievement and advancement. You will want to think about an ongoing advancement system. To fulfill this desire, I created a Model Team Certification Process. It consists of three increasing levels of competency each team can achieve: Main, Advanced, and Conductor (see Figure 8).

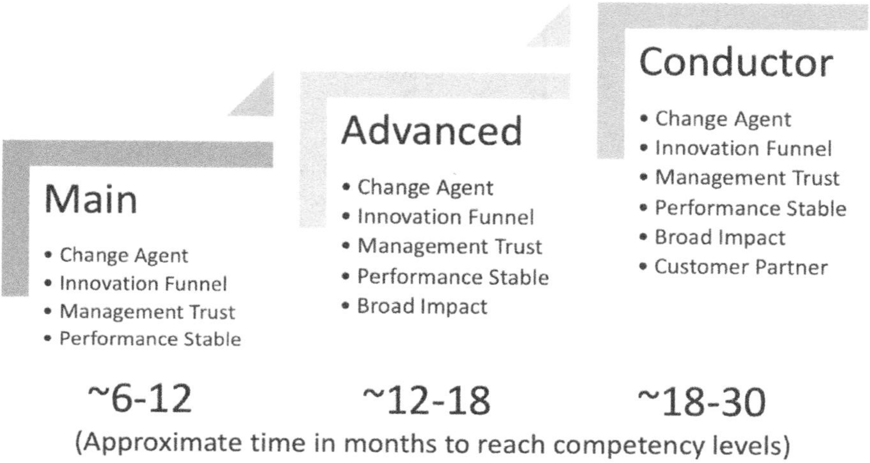

Main

- Change Agent
- Innovation Funnel
- Management Trust
- Performance Stable

Advanced

- Change Agent
- Innovation Funnel
- Management Trust
- Performance Stable
- Broad Impact

Conductor

- Change Agent
- Innovation Funnel
- Management Trust
- Performance Stable
- Broad Impact
- Customer Partner

~6-12   ~12-18   ~18-30

(Approximate time in months to reach competency levels)

Figure 8 – Model Team Certification Levels

To achieve the first level (Main) of certification, the Model Team must demonstrate competency in the following four key areas with the specified weight of each to the overall score (see Figure 9):

- Change Leadership 30%
- Employee Ideas and Innovation 30%
- Visual Management with Huddles 20%
- Performance 20%

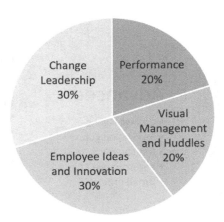

Figure 9 – Model Team Main Certification Components

Each of the four areas have specific measurable criteria assessed by your KPO and leadership team. (See appendix for a template.) A majority of weight (60% total) is applied to the elements of change leadership and employee ideas and innovation for a reason. There is only 20% of the total evaluation score for achieving performance, and 20% for cadence as measured through the metrics. This is designed to ensure a healthy balance between <u>what</u> the team achieves, and <u>how</u> they get there. As leaders, we want to ensure the right behavior, not just results, are present, in order to ensure lasting operational sustainability. We will have wasted our time if we put together a Model Team that achieves its performance metrics but does not manage the change well and/or fails to engage its team in innovation. There is no sustainability in this scenario.

First Level Certification: Main

Let's look at a hypothetical example of a Model Team seeking their first-level Main certification. I will refer to them as the "Middle-shifters." They have been a Model Team since they pitched their idea of reinventing the middle shift, working from 3 p.m. to 11 p.m., about six months ago. Their leader is a newer supervisor with a bit of a rebellious attitude among his peers, but he is irrefutably respected by his direct team. He has come from a technical support group to lead this frontline service team. His tech-savvy has established instant credibility. He works to turn his Model Team in the right direction. They bring great ideas to the forefront. One of them discovers upwards of eight tickets being generated for the same transaction when only two are required. This unnecessary work is adding up to tens of thousands of dollars in wasted labor, and customer frustration expressed in so many messages filling up their email boxes. This leader further articulates that the shift away from issuing so many tickets could help improve customer wait times. The team has reached a sustained level of higher performance, has a strong employee innovation culture, and has run huddles without fail.

The Middle-shifters submit their self-assessment to achieve certification to the KPO. Their application will be reviewed and then, if ready, passed to the leadership team for final approval. The KPO is familiar with the projects of the group and knows they have achieved a strong performance record. There is just one thing wrong. The change management required to adjust from eight tickets to two is missing. They have discovered a great opportunity and proved it could work. However, they have not socialized, nor operationalized it. This leader's fellow supervisors are skeptical of the process. The support group, where he came from, didn't know what was needed to implement it.

Change is hard, and it can take time. Time is not something extra this supervisor has in abundance. What he does have is recurring weekly program reviews with a large audience, a KPO with resources, and a group of colleagues who would gladly help him, if he asked. The KPO puts the application on hold and turns to coach this Middle-shifter supervisor. They help him to put his team's idea into a brief to be shared at the next weekly review with a specific request for the help they need to translate it into action. They get the unwavering agreement from the support team to lead the evaluation of excessive tickets. With this data now available, other supervisors become aware of the time their team is wasting. This leads to a systemic change in the workflow of multiple groups across the enterprise.

We didn't expect an enterprise-wide impact as big as the one the Middle-shifters delivered. Nor did we expect this supervisor and his team to own the entire process of redesign and deployment. What we did expect, and our KPO coached for, was the demonstrated ability to manage a change. With just a simple request for help, and socializing using data, it turned out to be a grand solution.

When we and our teams demonstrate full engagement in a repeatable and transferable way, then we have the foundation to achieve a high-performing world-class operation. The Middle-shifters will now achieve their first-level Model Team Main Certification and you celebrate with perhaps a small gathering of cake and coffee. Each of the teammates has a new swing in their step. They have made it to the top of the first summit gaining marketable skills along the way.

Second Level Certification: Advanced

Reaching the Advanced stage requires an emphatic understanding, translation, and sharing of Model Team skills to bring broader value to the organization. It specifically requires the Model Team leader and their group to take it up a notch by seeking out larger-impact and typically more difficult projects. This means a demonstration of an improvement project conducted with and for the benefit of multiple teams. This will typically require a multi-day Kaizen event facilitated by your KPO. The advanced certification can only be achieved after the main level one is complete. The advanced level provides far-reaching scalability to other parts of the organization.

Let's play out another scenario for this one. You have a team ready to reach the Advanced level of Model Team certification. This group has initiated a large improvement effort involving multiple departments within the company. It was born from one employee's ideas to improve interdepartmental communication. This team is in the hot seat when it comes to providing answers to customers' inquiries about overdue orders. When the answer to the updated delivery date is not found in the system, but with an employee in another department who is unreachable, these customer service reps get antsy. They have thought of all kinds of possibilities, from two-way radios to paging systems to resolve the communication connection problem.

Any solution offered would need to be adopted by a department across towns, states, and the nation. Getting the other departments to participate in the improvement project was imperative in order to make real change. The supervisor and their manager brought the problem statement to the other department's leadership and frontline. They shared real customer cases and data. They invited them to be part of the week-long event. The supervisor worked with her leadership team, and gave you a heads up of the problem at hand too, asking for support.

The supervisor and one of her reps take part in a week-long Kaizen facilitated event along with the other department's personnel. Both teams are updated during the event and participate in some of the try-storming exercises (refer to Chapter 4). The camaraderie, not to mention, communication between the departments is excellent. It doesn't end at the conclusion of the Kaizen event. The solution the teams chose includes mobile phones on the production floor allowing them to "hot-line" employee to employee for real-time answers to the most urgent of customer inquiries. This bridge of customer needs to the production crew brings a new external focus for all. It shows that every employee can bring positive change forward when they work together, across the broader organization.

Third Level Certification: Conductor

Conductor level certification is the third level. It requires the attainment of main and advanced certifications, plus a significant positive improvement directly for and with external customers. While all levels of Model Teams will improve the customers' experience in some fashion, this one requires significant communication and planning skills to seek out innovation relating to some of the biggest headaches clients (and your business) have. It also involves bringing customers directly in on the problem, and solution. As with the previous level, achievement typically requires a full week of Kaizen. I have seen transformational outcomes such as new enterprise-wide mobile applications come to fruition in the pursuit of this level.

The highest level of achievement proves, beyond a shadow of a doubt, that the leader and their team are ready to move on to higher levels of responsibility. Get ready because they will probably want to. You may find that, at this point, your leaders are highly sought after to lead other parts of the company. This is exactly what you were hoping for. Lead your team and help them prosper. You can refer to the appendix for a template and example of the main certification level requirements. Contact me for info on certification at higher levels, or visit www.ModelTeamEnterprises.com.

Leveling Up a Model Team

How do you decide when a Model Team is ready to move on to the next level and become certified? An outline of skills and behaviors needed should give you a good guide to follow. Ultimately, your leadership team will hold decision-making authority. Personally, I choose to be in the approval loop because I thoroughly enjoy coaching teams, seeing their successes, and understanding their struggles. I also do it to demonstrate care, concern, and commitment to the integrity of the program. The way you spend your time with the team will speak volumes about what you care about and the results you achieve.

One point I know can be challenging for employees and leaders is when roles change, especially within the departments. Folks will want to know that, once they are certified, their achievement carries over with them to a new team and/or role. Admittedly, the team who achieved the Main certification level may not have the same folks still on it when it applies for the Advanced level. The demographic of frontline teams can change a lot in a year. It is important to recognize the skills of each member in relation to the team as a whole. You may have experienced supervisors who achieve Advanced level and then take on a new group that is in need of basic training. The supervisor's new team can get to the Main certification level faster, but it is not a given. It's not the person; it's the team as a whole to whom the standards are applied.

How exactly does a Model Team get from shark tank to certification? They

126

get there by investing in training, coaching, setting key performance metrics, operating rhythms, streamlining, and engaging in innovation of their work processes. Fundamentally, we have to put the time and discipline into how things work. This is no different from any other achievement we strive for in our professional or personal lives. Set goals, and set up a training regime. Practice, practice, and more practice. Compete, learn, and adjust. Win.

Model Team Methodology™ works because nearly everyone has a competitive nature and likes to achieve goals. This is especially true of business-minded people. Think back to Chapter 1. The first two Model Teams asked to go on the journey. They each wanted to be first to be recognized, rewarded, and promoted. Were there some supervisors who simply shunned the idea of participating and stayed out of the fray? Yes, honestly, I have seen a few who either outright refused to come to the shark tank session or were coincidentally ill or otherwise indisposed on the date of the session. Eventually, they didn't make it within the organization. The standards I set did not tolerate this behavior. Instead, I recognized and rewarded those who were willing to engage themselves and their team in innovating for the future. It is simply more fun to be on a winning team, with a feeling of excitement for the unknown. For the entrepreneurs, engineers, and especially service people who love to troubleshoot, discovery is a fun zone. Recognize, reward, and promote those who have the courage to lead through ambiguity.

"The reward for work well done is the opportunity to do more." – Jonas Salk

Reward icon: Freepik via Flaticon.com

Model Leader Reflection–Recognize, Reward, Promote

1. What behaviors and deliverables have you recognized your team for?
2. Do you have a recognition plan and is it transparent to all?
3. Have you outlined a clear path to advancement for your team?
4. As you embark on your Model Team journey, what can you see the team achieving as they reach a higher level?

Chapter 12

Lessons Learned... Adaptation Feeds Wisdom

We learn more from failure than we do success, or so the saying goes. Failure is dreadful and painful, yet it is a reality of life. The Center for Management & Organization Effectiveness[49] highlights a few of the reasons why teams fail, including heated conflicts, resistance to change, and failure to innovate. They point to noteworthy examples of teams going from the top to bottom that are worthy of study including the LA Lakers, Sears, and Oldsmobile.

First, consider the LA Lakers. They were on top of their game, winning three straight NBA championships from 2000-2002. Then they drafted two talented Type A players; Shaquille O'Neal and Kobe Bryant. The pair were both stubborn and they could not get along. The coaches began fighting and made bad trades. The rest of the team faced extended injuries as uncertainty loomed. In these conditions, it's hard to win. As leaders, if we are constantly frustrated, and let contentious relationships fester, our teams will not succeed.

Then there is Sears, the leading retailer for much of the twentieth century. It was a beloved store for my family, where we would shop for new school clothes, appliances, and tools we still use to this day. Beginning in 1999, the big box home improvement stores and blooming online retailers posed a serious challenge to Sears. Despite their huge brand name recognition and value, and the fact they had home shopping and delivery via their catalog before anyone else, Sears retreated. They closed stores and reduced marketing spend. They needed to make a bold change, but they did not. Today, they are a skeleton of their former brand.

Thirdly, Oldsmobile was founded in 1897 and was considered GM's innovation brand. They had so many firsts in the automobile industry, including the first fully automatic transmission, front-wheel drive, and airbags. Yet somehow innovation stopped, and new designs faltered. They ignored what the rest of the world was focusing on; fuel efficiency. They lost their competitive edge and simply stopped innovating.

I share these examples because they are all industries where Model Team Methodology™ could have helped alleviate the losses. Whether a sports team, a retailer, a manufacturing company, or any other enterprise where leadership and teamwork matter, the building blocks of Model Teams are foundational. Like anything in life though, while I have had successes, I can't pretend there weren't mistakes and missteps along the way, so let me explain some of them.

Be Patient or Learn How

I knew it would be risky to take on a green field start-up project in a dirt floor warehouse in a foreign country. I had no prior manufacturing experience, and only knew a few phrases in Spanish... and they were mostly the bad ones. Alas, I did follow my gut and go south of the US border. I learned how to build circuit boards by filling in as the second shift supervisor at the headquarters plant while planning the start-up. I hired well, built quality products, and created a productive and playful environment. There were daily huddles with clear metrics. Accountability was never in question. There was high care and concern. But, I was impatient. I tried to do Model Teams everywhere and all at once. I pushed to get every team in the plant to follow the new way, whether it fitted them or not. I was prioritizing standardization, to gain efficiency, above local intel. Making progress was harder than it needed to be. It was nearly impossible to achieve lasting results in all the teams. It would be years later before I learned to treat transformation less like L.A. traffic and more like a cross-country trip. Plan your route, expect road construction, and stop to take in the local flavor and scenery every chance you get.

'Patience is a virtue and a skill'

Listen, Visualize, and Follow Up

Next, leading a back-office team provided a lesson in transforming work that was hard to see. Most of it was hidden in computers and file cabinets. By visualizing the work and setting audacious goals the team achieved more than 140% improvement in contract processing turnaround time, reduced invoicing errors, and improved receivables and cash flow significantly. The transformation was a true success, yet the sales team hated the rigidity of some of the new processes. Their deal creativity had been suppressed in favor of scalability. The frontline idea mechanisms were not robust. We had been listening to the team right in front of us in the office, but not enough to the frontline in the field with customers. Or, maybe it was that we listened, but the field inputs were distantly modulated and/or we failed consistently to share the results of the impact and effort assessment with them. My lesson here was to ensure frontline innovation is approached systemically with 100% follow-up.

Engage the Frontline to Make Lasting Change

Lastly, I have also learned to prioritize working root causes with the most valuable return on investment and to allow time for them to come to fruition. In my time working in field and call center service, I have witnessed really upset customers and employees. There was always a myriad of reasons why things went awry and blame to go with it. I had to fight the tendency to lean toward that "one throat to choke" mantra. Blaming someone never resolved anything. Regardless of what was wrong, I looked toward the team to help me find real root causes of the most pressing concerns.

It can take several months to see improvement. There were times when my team slid backward due to hiring freezes and untimely operational delays. I found some managers and supervisors hijack the daily huddles in favor of their own ideas or cancel them because they didn't want to lose the nine minutes of operational time due to the weight of wanting to make their metrics. I got mad when I heard about this, but I also knew I was part of the problem. If I pushed the metrics too hard, too fast, there was no room to breathe. I also knew there were some leaders in the group who would not adapt to the new mode and I had to let them go. However, my biggest learning from this was to keep on keeping on. The system works as long as you keep on going. Don't stop. Don't mix up the steps. Don't doubt yourself. Don't ask for permission. Get the right players on the bus. Engage the frontline in innovation, as this is where the best ideas are for enabling prosperity for your business.

One Step At a Time

Even with the best-laid plans, you can count on a major crisis to upend them. During the recent global pandemic, it felt like there was a 500-pound weight on my chest. But, I had to remind myself that I had survived hurricanes, floods, tornadoes, earthquakes, and riots. The crisis was temporary.

If you are feeling overwhelmed by a tsunami of your complex daily work, with no hope of transforming your team, you are not alone. It is not easy to navigate the chaos, but employing the Model Team Methodology™ can help you regain your sanity by making a step-wise change that leads to prosperity and longevity. You see, what kept the teams and I strong through each of these experiences was a deep belief in the power of positive thinking, coupled with a one-step-at-a-time approach. I am not sure where the saying, "You can't eat an elephant all at once," comes from, but it's a good analogy here. Especially in recent years, I knew we had made the right investment in our people. I knew we had the right metrics and accountability. We just needed to change our workout routines so they could be done differently. As a triathlete, it was a real bummer when all the pools closed during the pandemic. I had to switch solely to dry-land training to maintain muscle mass. The same could be said for those working completely remotely. Don't give up on your operating mechanisms; instead, adapt them. Make them shorter. Record short videos to share key messages. I did one from my home office wearing a ball cap and frankly chuckled at how much I needed a haircut. It wasn't staged. I didn't have any communications help or an editor. It was just me being me.

Like my team, I was simply showing I was human in the absence of a normal that was not going to be there anymore. I recognized we had to create a new normal. My success in making it through each crisis was based on continuous transparent communication and reliance on our core foundation of working as a team we could model others after. This is what Model Team Methodology™ is all about: proving to yourself and your team you can set goals and achieve them by engaging the team in innovation, even if you stumble and fail along the way. After all, failure is part of growth. I have personally known some folks who never truly recovered from being knocked down, fired, or lost. However, I have seen more rise up and do better than before. I suppose I tend to hang out with the more optimistic crowd anyway. The point is to recognize failure, learn from it, and use the knowledge to become better.

Career growth icon image: Kalashnyk via Flaticon.com

Model Leader Reflection–Learning Who You Are

1. What hasn't gone the way you wanted it to?
2. Are there learnings you can reflect on from this experience?
3. Is patience a strength or a liability for you?
4. How can you be gentler on yourself?

Chapter 13

Go Forth and Remember... Deciding and Doing are Not the Same Thing

An old riddle:

Five Frogs are sitting on a log.
    Four decide to jump off.
    How many are left?
    Five.
    The answer is five, because deciding and doing are not the same thing.[50]

'Understand deciding and doing are not the same thing'

I have transformed many operations, enabling them to gain efficiencies, improve the bottom line, make work easier, and add more value for customers. You can do it too. Whether you are in a crisis right now, sick of the status quo, or on top of your game, you instinctively know you need to innovate to get ahead and stay ahead. Your team needs you to engage them. Here's how we create a sustainable operation that will continually innovate and transform itself beyond our wildest expectations.

1. **Select** a small team (say 5 to 30 people with a single leader) who will become a proof point for what great looks like. This will be the first Model Team. We can create additional teams as resources and operational stability allow.
2. **Train** this team on how to look for waste, generate ideas and solutions, and work together to improve the customer and employee experience.
3. **Instill** daily operating huddles with this team, and a weekly program review with the KPO. Ensure the discipline of regular cadence does not waver. Lead by example by dedicating our time and being fully engaged in the reviews.
4. **Visualize** metrics for the team. Tell them what performance measures we expect and inspect them. Make the goals clearly known and obvious

for all to see in a common dashboard format. This can be a whiteboard in the office, or on a digital sketchpad via video call. Don't harp on about missing the metrics. Coach for progress, not perfection.

5. **Ideate** with employees constantly and follow through 100% on every idea submitted. Be inclusive of the assessment of effort versus business impact. Involve them in the implementation. We will get more ideas than we can handle. Many will be transformational. Listen to and elicit frontline ideas emphatically.

6. **Coach** change leadership. This is our main job. We cannot assume it will happen because everyone chooses the best idea and solution to implement. Things will go wrong. Fail fast, learn, and adapt. Provide air cover for the team. Manage the inevitable change curve for the shortest dip and duration possible. Do more than decide. Get stuff done.

7. **Recognize, Reward, and Promote** with clarity the behaviors and performance that make our business prosper. Remember that recognition and reward are not the same things. Recognition is not expensive. Promotion is the ultimate reward for a job well done. Make work fun and develop our people.

None of what I have outlined is really hard. We just need to commit to our team to provide them with better work environments so they can provide better service and products to our customers. In the end, we will find the culture we create feeding itself. An inspiring workplace comes into being. Our team wants to work there. They do not tolerate sloppy processes. They hunger for learning and development. The system craves and attracts nourishment, with continuous challenge and change. With high accountability and equally high care and concern ever present, we can make a great employee experience equate to a great customer experience. This will lead to better profits every single time.

So, how many employees does it take to change a lightbulb? The answer... just one. The one who recognizes the light is out, knows having it on is better, has the skill to change it, and is empowered to do so.

Leadership icon image: Becris via Flaticon.com

Epilogue

Frequently Asked Questions

Q: Do we have to start a Model Team to make the employee innovation system work?

A: Based on my experience, we will be more successful if we start innovating with a focused group, who have clear metrics, disciplined operating metrics, proper training, and program management support. I have seen other methods of employee innovation work, but generally they are neither sustainable nor scalable for the aforementioned reasons.

Q: Does Model Team Methodology™ only work in organizations with multiple teams doing the same kind of work, such as call centers, or can it work in a one-department firm, such as engineering for example?

A: The great thing about Model Team Methodology™ is how adaptable it is to various types of companies and teams. The premise is to cultivate a focused team, a team we want to model others on, and move forward from there. I have personally created Model Teams in manufacturing, financial, and service operations. I have seen pieces of it applied in engineering teams, specifically the continuous improvement and Six Sigma tools facilitated by a Kaizen Promotion Office (KPO). If we lead a small team today, we start there.

If we have multiple teams doing various types of work, we start with the one who wants to be, and can be the model for the others. By engaging our team in innovation and providing clear goals for them, we can have a positive impact on employee and customer experience, and thus deliver for our company.

Q: You often mention reliance on the Kaizen Promotion Office. What if I we do not have one, nor the ability to fund one?

A: The KPO can be one individual we train for this purpose. Perhaps we can promote one of our best team leads or supervisors to take the role. There is a ton of training available to give them the skills. It is worth the investment and will be a clear sign to your organization of the transformation required. Feel free to call me for guidance.

Q: Should supervisors regularly engage in direct observation of employees at work regularly?

A: Absolutely, any leader who is directing work needs to take the time to observe directly what their team is being asked to do directly. This is not a micromanagement thing. It is about seeking to understand and showing keen interest in the employee and customer experience.

Templates

Model Team Selection Scoresheet (Template 1)

Team	Adaptive to Change	Understand Model Team Purpose	Deliver Results	Want to succeed	Total Score	Presentation Highlights
#1: (ie: ACME)	3	5	1	5	14	(ie: they want it, but are currently struggling to deliver)
#2						
#3						
#4						

Template 1–Model Team Selection Scoresheet

For each team presenting in your "shark-tank" Model Team selection session, have each reviewer allocate points in increments of 1=weak, 3=good, or

5=great, for each element. Total the point values resulting in a range from 4 (minimum) to 20 (maximum.) Be prudent in allocating points to determine a clear winner. You may have more or less than 4 groups presenting. Tally the scoresheets from each reviewer and deliberate where ties may exist in order to choose the Model Team. Feel free to adjust as needed.

Impact vs. Effort Grid (Template 2)

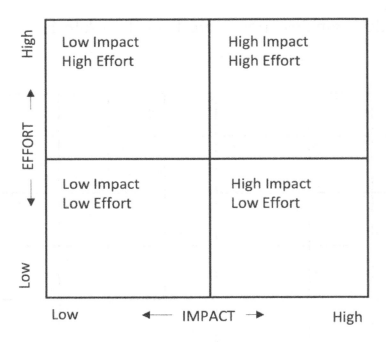

Template 2–Impact vs. Effort Grid

Prioritizing instructions: For any new idea or project, assess impact and effort in financial terms. Avoid subjective assessments. Do not get caught up in lengthy exacting estimates. Good enough is enough. Ideas placed in the top and bottom right-hand side boxes move forward. Those on the left-hand side are typically dismissed or bundled into more impactful changes in the future.

Certification Assessment–Main (Template 3a & 3b)

Model Team Name & Supervisor:		
Selection date:		
Most Significant Change(s) Made		
Scoring guide (0-25% = 1, 26-50% = 2, 51-75% = 3, 76%+ = 4)		
Innovation		
Percent of team submitting ideas		
Percent of ideas moved forward		
Team involvement in project implementation		
Innovation Total x 0.30		
Change Management		
Communication of changes		
Execution of changes		
Demonstration of wins		
Use of KPO/others to achieve objectives		
Change Management Total x 0.30		
Leadership		
Daily huddle cadence		
Huddle board updated and visible		
Teammates lead huddles		
Manager and team trust level		
Peer teams trust level		
Leadership Total x 0.20		
Business Performance		
Performance to scorecard metrics		
Business Performance Total x 0.20		
Total Score		
Notes:		

Template 3a–Model Team Certification Assessment–Level 1 Main

Model Team Name & Manager/Supervisor:		
Selection date:		
Most Significant Change(s) Made		
Scoring guide (0-25% = 1, 26-50% = 2, 51-75% = 3, 76%+ = 4)	Model Team Leader Asssessment	KPO Leader Assessment
Innovation		
Percent of team submitting ideas	2	2
Percent of ideas moved forward	2	2
Team involvement in project implementation	1	1
Innovation Total x 0.30	1.5	1.5
Change Management		
Communication of changes	4	3
Execution of changes	4	4
Demonstration of wins	4	3
Use of KPO/others to achieve objectives	4	4
Change Management Total x 0.30	4.8	4.2
Leadership		
Daily huddle cadence	4	4
Huddle board updated and visible	4	4
Teammates lead huddles	2	2
Manager and team trust level	3	3
Peer teams trust level	3	3
Leadership Total x 0.20	3.2	3.2
Business Performance		
Performance to scorecard metrics	4	4
Business Performance Total x 0.20	0.8	0.8
Total Score	10.3	9.7
Notes: 13.2 is highest possible score. 10.6 or higher is desired.	Ex: manager's score is ~ 78% grade. They might engage more employees in innovation to improve	Ex: KPO rated change lower and should coach the manager

Template 3b–Example: Model Team Certification Assessment–Level 1 Main

Assessment instructions: for a Model Team who has met their objectives (see Chapter 11 for more info) and wishes to apply for certification, they should consult with their manager and KPO lead first. When ready, the score sheet is completed by the Model Team supervisor/manager followed by the KPO Lead. Some of the sections are subjective. Utilize peer feedback and live observation to supplement ratings. If desired, the assessment and articles of completion, such as innovation charters, scorecards, etc., can be submitted to a board of review for final approval. A blank form and an example are provided below.

Operating Calendar (Template 4)

Daily	Weekly	Monthly	Quarterly	Semi-Annual	Annual

Template 4 – Operating Calendar

Suggested Operating Rhythms:

- Annual – Goal Setting
- Semi-Annual – Goal Checkup
- Quarterly – All Employee Town-halls, Customer and Business Reviews
- Monthly – Staff one-to-one
- Weekly – Innovation Funnel Review, Program Review, Performance Dashboard Review
- Daily – Stand-Up Session (Huddles)

Images and Illustrations

- Lightbulb Cover image and moment icon: Shutterstock.com
- Fishing icon image: Freepik via Flaticon.com https://www.flaticon.com/free-icon/fishing-rod-and-fisher_10965
- Diving icon image: Perkasa via Flaticon.com https://www.flaticon.com/free-icon/swimming_5481998?term=pool+diving&page=1&position=5&origin=search&related_id=5481998
- Team Learning icon: Eucaly.p via Flaticon.com https://www.flaticon.com/free-icon/team_1401931?term=team+learning&page=1&position=6&origin=search&related_id=1401931
- Planner icon image: Freepik via Flaticon.com https://www.flaticon.com/free-icon/weekly_5242701?term=planner&page=1&position=14&origin=search&related_id=5242701
- Dashboard icon image: Eucaly.p via Flaticon.com https://www.flaticon.com/free-icon/dashboard_2329087?term=dashboard&page=1&position=6&origin=search&related_id=2329087
- Idea icon image: Freepik via Flaticon.com https://www.flaticon.com/free-icon/idea_2081238?term=employee+idea&page=1&position=12&origin=search&related_id=2081238
- Ambassador icon image: Noomtah via Flaticon.com https://www.flaticon.com/free-icon/presenter_8706381?term=ambassador&page=1&position=6&origin=search&related_id=8706381
- SystemChange icon: Parzival 1997 via Flaticon.com https://www.flaticon.com/free-icon/system_7521598?term=system+change&page=1&po

sition=1&origin=search&related_id=7521598
- Honesty icon image: Freepik via Flaticon.com https://www.flaticon.com/free-icon/honesty_9077962?term=honesty&page=1&position=6&origin=search&related_id=9077962
- Reward icon image: Freepik via Flaticon.com https://www.flaticon.com/free-icon/reward_2666513?term=recognition+and+rewards&page=1&position=1&origin=search&related_id=2666513
- Career growth icon image: Kalashnyk via Flaticon.com https://www.flaticon.com/free-icon/career_6894608term=personal+growth&page=1&position=2&origin=search&related_id=6894608
- Leadership icon image: Becris via Flaticon.com https://www.flaticon.com/free-icon/leadership_860398?term=leadership&page=1&position=11&origin=search&related_id=860398
- Theodore Roosevelt quote, goodreads.com, accessed Jan 19, 2023
- Peter Drucker quote, brainyquote.com accessed January 18, 2023
- George Washington Carver quote, brainyquote.com accessed January 18, 2023
- Thomas Edison quote, brainyquote.com accessed January 18, 2023
- Jonas Salk quote, brainyquote.com accessed Feb 6, 2023
- Figure 1 – Profit as a function of Employee and Customer Experience, proprietary content from ModelTeamEnterprises.com
- Figure 2 – Model Team Methodology™ Lifecycle, proprietary content from ModelTeamEnterprises.com
- Figure 3 – Example Kaizen Promotion Organization Structure proprietary content from ModelTeamEnterprises.com
- Figure 4 – Employee Innovation Cycle, proprietary content from ModelTeamEnterprises.com
- Figure 5 – Impact versus Effort Grid, adapted from *The Lean Six Sigma Pocket Toolbook*, McGraw-Hill, 2005 pgs 264
- Figure 6 – Diffusion of Innovation Adoption Curve, *Diffusion of Innovations* by Everett Rogers, 1962
- Figure 7 – Change curves, adapted from personal change acceleration experience

- Figure 8 – Model Team Certification Levels, proprietary content from ModelTeamEnterprises.com
- Figure 9 – Model Team Main Certification Levels, proprietary content from ModelTeamEnterprises.com
- Cover Lightbulbs Photo: Shutterstock.com
- Author Photo: Lauren King

Acknowledgements

We are the sum of our experiences in life. I feel extremely grateful for the investment of so many great leaders who spent time with me. At the risk of omitting someone, I am compelled to expressly thank Tom Dunham and Mike Lehman for believing I had a spark that would help build a new service model and wow an investor meeting in New York. To Paul Senski, Jim Zaput, Dave Southgate, Jannette Damron, Harbinder Johl, and Don Scott for being in the field service trenches with me. To Dee Mellor, Jim Mitchell, Sherri Mowery, Rebecca Serwatt, and Paula Clayton for their coaching, grace, and mentorship. To Mike Swinford, Rob Reilly, Adam Holton, Nate Bailey, and Rich Neff for a seat at the executive table. To Steve Gemmell for proving to me IT is not a department. To Jim Davis and Scott Jeffers for providing me with the opportunity to take big swings. To Steve Rusckowski, Zeynep Ton, and Felix Oberholzer-Gee for providing me with the ability to understand what it takes to create "Good Jobs" that provide long-lasting business value. To Michelle Ricardo, Jennifer Conley, and Mary Chesser for teaching me how to put the "human" into "human resources". To Dr. Michelle Robin, Becky Blades, and the KC Business Journal's Women Who Mean Business tribe for inspiring me to be the best version of myself. To Jerry Camacho, for your love and patience, and for being my very best friend.

Notes

PREFACE

1   Fortune Magazine. 2022. *100 Best Companies To Work For*. Fortune Media IP Limited.

2   Zeynep Ton, MIT Sloan School of Management. 2014. *The Good Jobs Strategy*, 15-16. Houghton Mifflin Harcourt and Amazon.

3   Zeynep Ton, MIT Sloan School of Management. 2023. *The Case for Good Jobs*. Harvard Business School.

CHAPTER 1

4   Mark Burnett. 2009-present. *Shark Tank*. American Broadcasting Corp (ABC).

5   Brene Brown. 2018. *Dare to Lead*,172-175. Random House.

6   Curt W. Coffman and Kathie Sorensen PH.D. 2013. *Culture Eats Strategy for Lunch: The Secret of Extraordinary Results, Igniting the Passion Within*, 25-30. The Coffman Organization Inc.

CHAPTER 2

7   ASQ.org: https://asq.org/quality-resources/six-sigma/tools

8   Henry A. Landsberger. 1958. *Hawthorne Revisited*, Cornell University.

9   Matthew Dixon, Nick Toman, and Rick Delisi. 2013. *The Effortless Experience*. The Penguin Group.

10   Jeanne Bliss. 2012. *Chief Customer Officer*, 101-115. Josey Bass.

11   Zeynep Ton, Cate Reavis, and Sarah Kalloch. 2017. *MIT Sloan Case Study Quest Diagnostics*. https://goodjobsinstitute.org/portfolio/good-job-strategy-at-quest-diagnostics/

12   Amy Edmondson and Mark Mortensen. Jan-Feb 2023 *Rethink your employee value proposition*, Harvard Business Review.

CHAPTER 3

13   Graban and Schwartz . 2013. *The Executive Guide to Healthcare Kaizen: Leadership for a Continuously Learning and Improving Organization*, 138-139. CRC Press, Taylor & Francis Group.

14   Womack and Jones. 1996. *Lean Thinking*, 23. Simon and Schuster.

15   Shingijutsu Lean Consulting Company. http://www.shingijutsu-global.com/en/index.html

CHAPTER 4

16 Lean Enterprise Institute. https://www.lean.org/

17 William Wiggenhorn. 1990. *Motorola U.* HBR Magazine.

18 Erica Keswin. 2022. *3 Ways to Boost Retention Through Professional Development.* Harvard Business Review.

19 David Drickhamer. 2022. *To Successfully Apply Lean Thinking in Distribution, Go to Where the Action Is!* The Lean Enterprise Institute: https://www.lean.org

CHAPTER 5

20 Curt W. Coffman and Kathie Sorensen PH.D.. 2013. *Culture Eats Strategy for Lunch: The Secret of Extraordinary Results, Igniting the Passion Within,* 25-30. The Coffman Organization Inc.

CHAPTER 6

21 John Womack & Daniel T. Jones. 1996. *Lean Thinking,* 94-98, 261-62, 306-7, 309. Simon and Schuster.

22 Chris McChesney, Sean Covey, and Jim Huling. 2018. *4 Disciplines of Execution.* Simon and Schuster.

23 Weight Watchers program: https://www.weightwatchers.com/

24 Stephan Kudyba and Agnel D'Cruz. 2021. *Building a Better Dashboard for Your Agile Project.* Harvard Business Review.

25 Felix Oberholzer-Gee. 2021. *Better, Simpler, Strategy,* 174-77. Harvard Business School.

CHAPTER 7

26 Naz Beheshti. 2019. *10 Timely Statistics About The Connection Between Employee Engagement And Wellness.* Gallup study published on https://www.forbes.com/.

27 Felix Oberholzer-Gee. 2021. *Better Simpler Strategy,* 117-22. Harvard Business School.

28 John Kotter. 1996. *Leading Change.* Harvard Business School Press.

29 Jeff Dyer, Nathan Furr, Curtis Lefrandt, and Taeya Howell. 2023. *Why Innovation Depends on Intellectual Honesty.* MIT Sloan Review.

30 Fabrizio Salvador and Fabian J. Sting. 2022. *How Your Company Can Encourage Innovation from All Employees.* Harvard Business Review.

31 Gartner® Inc Technological Research and Consulting firm: www.gartner.com

CHAPTER 8

32 Wayne Baker. 2016. *The More You Energize Your Coworkers, the Better Everyone Performs.* Harvard Business Review.

33 Jon Michail. 2020. *Strong Nonverbal Skills Matter Now More Than Ever In This "New Normal.* Forbes https://www.forbes.com/

34 Marie Mitchell. 2017. *Why do employees cheat? Too much pressure.* Science Daily University of Georgia.

CHAPTER 9

35 Alan Deutschman. 2007. *Change or Die.* Harper Collins.

36 John Kotter. 1996. *Leading Change, 20-3.* Harvard Business School Press.

37 William Barnett, Glenn Carroll, Victoria Chang. 2001. *Agilent Technologies: Organizational Change (A & B).*

38 Mark Feldman and Michael Spratt. 1998. *Five Frogs on a Log,* 29-30, 71, 148. PriceWaterhouseCoopers and Harper Collins.

39 Everett Rogers. 1962 revised in 2003. *Diffusion of Innovation.* Free Press.

40 Tricia Emerson. 2022. *The Performance Dip Myth.* Forbes.com.

41 David Wilkinson. 2016. *Is the change curve a myth?* https://oxford-review.com/is-the-change-curve-real/

CHAPTER 10

42 Patrick Lencioni. 2002. *Five Dysfunctions of A Team,* 195-215. Jossey Bass

43 Microsoft. Sep 22, 2022. *Work Trend Index: Hybrid Work Is Just Work. Are We Doing It Wrong?* https://www.microsoft.com/en-us/worklab/work-trend-index/

44 Scott Berkun. 2013. *The Year Without Pants,* 29- 42. Jossey Bass

CHAPTER 11

45 Tribeca Productions and Everyman Pictures. 2004. *Meet the Fockers.* Scene available at https://www.youtube.com/watch?v=x-A6zERn6yo

46 Ash Carter. May 23, 2017. *What I learned from transforming the US Military approach to talent.* Harvard Business Review.

47 Bob Nelson, Ph.D. 2012. *1501 Ways to Reward Employees,* 7, 41. Workman Publishing.

48 Project Management Institute. https://www.pmi.org › project-management-pmp

CHAPTER 12

49 Center for Management and Organizational Effectiveness. Accessed July 1, 2023. *5 Teams That Failed to Stay Afloat (And What Sank Them).* Site Blog: https://cmoe.com/blog/big-teams-that-failed/

CHAPTER 13

50 Mark Feldman and Michael Sprat. 1998. *Five Frogs on a Log.* PriceWaterhouseCoopers and HarperCollins.

About the Author

MaryAnn Camacho is the CEO and Founder of Model Team Enterprises, a consulting firm helping business leaders engage employees through innovation. With over 30 years of Senior Executive experience in Corporate America, she is actively engaged in speaking, authoring, mentoring, and several entrepreneurial ventures. She has been featured in work at MIT Sloan School of Management, Harvard Business School Online, and in multiple publications by renowned fellows. She was named by the Kansas City Business Journal as the Top 25 Women Who Mean Business in 2019. She spends her spare time training and competing in triathlons. MaryAnn lives with her husband and son in Kansas.

You can connect with me on:
- https://modelteamenterprises.com
- https://twitter.com/MACamacho19
- https://www.facebook.com/100071968266532

Made in the USA
Monee, IL
20 February 2024

53791669R10095